D1219768

Magic Chef Cooking

Prepared and Tested in the
Research Kitchen of

AMERICAN STOVE COMPANY
at CLEVELAND, OHIO

under the direction of

DOROTHY E. SHANK, M. A.

formerly Instructor of
Food Research, Household Arts Department
Teachers College, Columbia University
New York City

Price, One Dollar

American Stove Company
St. Louis, Mo.

COPYRIGHT 1935

by American Stove Company

First Edition . . . . *November 1924*
Second Edition . . . . *April 1925*
Third Edition . . . . *May 1926*
Fourth Edition . . . . *September 1926*
Fifth Edition . . . . *August 1927*
Sixth Edition . . . . *July 1928*
Seventh Edition . . . . *June 1929*
Eighth Edition . . . . *August 1930*
Ninth Edition . . . . *December 1931*
Tenth Edition . . . . *November 1933*
Eleventh Edition . . . . *June 1934*
Twelfth Edition . . . . *August 1935*
Thirteenth Edition . . . . . . *February 1936*

Printed and Bound in the U.S.A. by
KINGSPORT PRESS, Inc., Kingsport, Tennessee

CONTENTS

3

CONTENTS

ILLUSTRATIONS

PREFACE

The purpose of the Lorain Oven Heat Regulator is to maintain a constant temperature during any baking period. The element of uncertainty in guessing the temperature and controlling the gas flow by hand is eliminated. The use of this device assures uniform products each time a given recipe is baked. It saves watching the food while it bakes, as has to be done when there is no control on the stove. This, of course, saves time, releasing the homemaker for other work.

The use of the Lorain Oven Heat Regulator also eliminates burning of food which may happen when one has to regulate the oven by hand adjustment of the gas cocks. It is practically impossible to make this adjustment by hand for any specific temperature even though a thermometer is used, for the temperature of the oven soon goes beyond the point desired. Or, the oven is apt to cool too much and the food will not bake as quickly as it should.

Directions for Using the Red Wheel

The Lorain Oven Heat Regulator, the first thermostatic control to be placed on a gas range, automatically controls the flow of gas to the oven burner, maintaining any desired baking temperature. It measures the heat, making Time and Temperature Cookery possible and easy.

At the side of the oven is a Red Wheel marked at intervals of 50 degrees Fahrenheit. It has half way points for every 25 degrees very plainly indicated, and smaller markings to indicate every 10 degrees.

Turn the Red Wheel until the temperature selected

is opposite the pointed indicator. Light the oven burner, turning the gas cock on to its full capacity. Preheat the oven until the desired temperature has been reached. The flow of gas will be automatically reduced when the oven registers the temperature at which the Red Wheel has been set. The length of time for the oven to reach the desired temperature varies with gas in different localities, different sizes of ovens, and different temperatures. A little experience and observation will be helpful in learning to know how long the oven burner should be lighted before the oven is to be used.

The pilot light on all Lorain equipped stoves should be kept burning whenever the oven is lighted. If the gas pressure becomes very low the pilot light may be extinguished. Therefore, it must be watched as the pilot light must be kept constantly burning. The pilot light should burn with a flame about an inch long whenever the oven is in use. If the stove is equipped with a clock attachment the pilot light should burn constantly. If, because of incomplete combustion, it should become slightly clogged a small wire may be used to clean the opening.

After the food has been placed in the oven and the door closed, let it remain undisturbed until time to remove it. Follow the Time and Temperature suggested in this recipe book.

Lorain Cooking

The purpose of this book is to present as many types of recipes as possible with proper baking Times and Temperatures for use in Lorain Controlled Ovens. Other recipes using other proportions may require a slight change in the length of baking time.

PREFACE

Pans of varying sizes and materials make a difference in results and, therefore, variations in the baking time may be desirable. Individual preference and differences in brands and grades of ingredients, may affect the result from time to time.

The Times and Temperatures given in the recipes in this book are suggested merely to serve as guides. They give a wide enough range in time to allow for most circumstances. When a satisfactory Time and Temperature is found for the conditions in each home, repeat it each time the recipe is tried.

All of the recipes in this book have been tested in the Research Kitchen of American Stove Company.

Use standard measuring cups and spoons when preparing them. Measure all ingredients accurately. *Use level measures.* Sift white flour once before measuring. If the flour has become damp from moisture absorbed, it should be dried by sifting in front of a warm oven before using.

Never bake directly on the bottom of the oven. Always place the pan on one of the grates which should be adjusted a few inches from the bottom of the oven. The center of the oven is usually the best position for baking. With the Lorain Oven Heat Regulator the oven temperature is uniform throughout the oven.

Never use baking sheets which will cover the entire surface of the grate. This will baffle the heat and prevent circulation of the heated air. Allow at least two inches around the edge of the oven. If two sheets are to be used the products on both sheets will not be evenly baked because the lower sheet will diffuse the heat and the top sheet will not get as much as it should have for even baking.

It is better to keep one temperature for the entire length of time wherever possible as in this way it is

PREFACE

unnecessary to have the baking constantly in mind.
It can be forgotten from the time it goes into the oven
until the time for it to be removed. However, in some
instances two temperatures may facilitate the preparation of whole meals or may be necessary in order not
to sacrifice the quality of the product.

MAGIC CHEF COOKING

CHAPTER I

YEAST BREADS

It will be best to find a satisfactory kind of flour for bread making; determine the amount to use for good results under the given circumstances, then always try to use the same amount of the same kind of flour.

Plain Breads

YEAST BREAD

Temperature, 450 degrees; Time, 15 minutes
then
Temperature, 375 degrees; Time, 45 minutes
or
Temperature, 375 degrees; Time, 1 hour

1 cake compressed yeast	7 cups flour
1 tablespoon sugar	½ tablespoon salt
1 pint liquid	2 tablespoons fat

The liquid used in this recipe may be either milk or water. If water is used boil it and then let it cool to a lukewarm temperature. If milk is used—and milk adds to the food value of your bread—scald it and then let it cool to a lukewarm temperature.

Crumble the yeast into a mixing bowl and add the sugar. Add the lukewarm liquid to the yeast mixture. Stir well to mix the ingredients thoroughly, then add about half of the flour which has been measured after sifting once, and the salt. The temperature of the flour should be about 90 degrees Fahrenheit.

Add the melted fat after about one half of the flour has been added. This prevents a streak of fat through the bread. Beat this batter thoroughly and add the remainder of the flour gradually. Different brands and grades of flour will take up different amounts of liquid. Mix the dough until all of the flour necessary to make a stiff dough has been worked in. It may require more or less than the 7 cups given in the recipe. Remove it to a floured board or clean table top and knead until it is smooth and elastic. This will take from 5 to 10 minutes.

Let the dough rise in a clean covered bowl until it is double in bulk, keeping it at a lukewarm temperature during the entire time of rising. This can be easily accomplished by keeping the bread covered in a bowl surrounded by warm water. It will take about 2 hours for the bread to rise. When the dough has risen until double in bulk remove from the bowl and again knead on a slightly floured board for about 5 minutes.

Shape it into 2 loaves and put it into well-greased bread pans. Cover them with a clean cloth and let rise again until double in bulk, keeping the temperature as already given. This will take about 1 hour. Then set the Red Wheel at 450 degrees and bake for 15 minutes, then 375 degrees for 45 minutes longer. Or, it may be baked at 375 degrees for 1 hour. Cool, uncovered, on cake racks.

Yield: Two 4½ x 8½ inch loaves or
Two smaller loaves and a few biscuits.

* * * *

The method of making Graham or whole wheat bread is the same as for white bread but usually one half the amount of flour used is white flour. A loaf of a smaller volume and coarser texture will result when all Graham or whole wheat flour is used. Graham or whole wheat flour also will vary in composition due to milling conditions.

GRAHAM OR WHOLE WHEAT BREAD

Temperature, 450 degrees; Time, 15 minutes
then
Temperature, 375 degrees; Time, 40 to 45 minutes

1 cake compressed yeast	3½ cups Graham or whole
1 tablespoon sugar	wheat flour
2 cups milk, scalded	1 tablespoon salt
3½ cups white flour	2 tablespoons fat

PARKER HOUSE ROLLS MAY BE SERVED AT ANY MEAL

HOT MUFFINS FOR BREAKFAST ARE ENTICING

Mix this according to the directions given for mixing white bread, but do not sift the Graham or whole wheat flour. Bake at 450 degrees for 15 minutes, then at 375 degrees for 40 to 45 minutes.

Two tablespoons of molasses may be used instead of the sugar. This will produce a loaf of a darker color and will change the flavor. One cup of seeded raisins may also be added, if desired.

Yield: Two 4½ x 8½ inch loaves, or
Two smaller loaves and a few biscuits.

*   *   *   *

Fancy Breads

RAISIN BREAD

Temperature, 375 degrees; Time, 50 minutes

1 cup milk	4 cups flour
1 cake compressed yeast	4 tablespoons fat
4 tablespoons sugar	1½ cups raisins
1½ teaspoons salt	

Scald the milk. Crumble the yeast with the sugar in a bowl. When the milk is lukewarm add it to the yeast and sugar mixture. Add the salt and half of the flour. Add the fat, which has been melted, and the raisins. Add the remaining flour. Knead until smooth and elastic. Place in a greased bowl and let rise until double in bulk. Shape into rolls. Let rise again and bake in a greased loaf pan at 375 degrees for 50 minutes.

Yield: 1 loaf 4½ x 8½ inches and a few biscuits.

TEA BRAID

Temperature, 400 degrees; Time, 30 to 35 minutes

1 cup milk, scalded
1 cake compressed yeast
4 tablespoons sugar
4 cups flour

1½ teaspoons salt
1 egg
4 tablespoons fat

Glazing

1 egg yolk
½ teaspoon milk

½ cup almonds

Use the same method for mixing as for bread, adding the beaten egg after part of the flour has been added. After the mixture has risen divide it into three pieces of equal size and roll between the hands and the unfloured board into long narrow strips of uniform size. Press together at one end and then braid. Put on a buttered sheet or pan, cover, and let rise. Brush with the yolk of 1 egg, slightly beaten and diluted with ½ teaspoon of cold milk. Sprinkle with ½ cup of finely chopped blanched almonds. The dough may be made into 1 large tea braid or 2 small ones. Bake on greased baking sheets or pans at 400 degrees for 30 to 35 minutes for one large braid. For two small braids bake at 400 degrees for 25 minutes.

Yield: 1 large braid, or
2 small braids.

TEA RING

Temperature, 400 degrees; Time, 30 to 35 minutes

Use the recipe given for Tea Braid and instead of dividing the dough roll it out to ½-inch thickness. Spread with ½ cup of melted butter, 1 teaspoon of cinnamon, and ½ cup of sugar creamed together. Sprinkle with ½ cup of nut meats. Roll like a jelly roll, pressing the ends together in a ring. Cut with the scissors or sharp knife into pieces about an inch wide. Do not cut entirely through the dough so the rolls will be held together with a band of dough on the inside. Turn the rolls so the cut side will be up. Sprinkle with nuts, let rise, and bake on a greased baking sheet at 400 degrees for 30 to 35 minutes.

Yield: 1 large ring.

Rolls

Quite a wide variation in baking time is given for rolls because the best length of time will depend on the size of the rolls and whether they are to be baked closely packed or separated. Thick rolls will require a longer time for baking than thin ones.

Plain Rolls may be made using the regular bread dough, but as a rule they are improved if sweetened slightly more than for bread and made a little richer. Recipes for rolls may vary quite widely in the content of sugar and fat. Some will require egg, and some will use raisins, orange or lemon rind, nuts, or spice.

All of these variations in ingredients will make some differences in the flavor of the rolls. They may be shaped differently to suit individual whims, but in all cases the general method of mixing will remain the same.

Milk will make rolls of finer texture than if water is used. It also adds to the food value. The same directions for mixing should be followed as when making bread.

*   *   *   *

ROLLS

Temperature, 400 degrees; Time, 12 to 15 minutes

1 cup milk	3½ cups flour
1 cake compressed yeast	1½ teaspoons salt
2 tablespoons sugar	2 tablespoons fat

Mix according to the directions given for Yeast Bread. Rolls may be shaped by cutting them into small balls of uniform size and rolling between the hands and unfloured board into balls of dough large or small, as desired. Place them on greased pans, far enough apart so the rolls will not touch. Let rise until double in bulk. Bake at 400 degrees for 12 to 15 minutes. If packed in a pan close together bake at 350 degrees for 35 to 40 minutes for large rolls.

Yield: Twenty 2½-inch rolls.

CINNAMON ROLLS

Temperature, 400 degrees; Time, 20 to 25 minutes

1 cup milk
1 cake compressed yeast
4 tablespoons sugar

4 cups flour
1½ teaspoons salt
4 tablespoons fat

For Filling

¼ cup butter
½ cup brown sugar

1 teaspoon cinnamon

Mix as for Yeast Bread. After the dough has risen roll it out in a thin sheet about ¼ inch thick. Spread with the butter, brown sugar, and cinnamon which have been creamed together. Roll like a jelly roll and cut into pieces about 1½ inches wide. Place close together cut side down in a pan in which has been put another ¼ cup of butter and ½ cup of brown sugar. Let rise until double in bulk and bake at 400 degrees for 20 to 25 minutes. One half cup of pecan meats may be added to the sugar and butter if desired.

Yield: Eighteen to twenty 2½-inch rolls.

PARKERHOUSE ROLLS

Temperature, 400 degrees; Time, 15 to 20 minutes

1 cup milk
1 cake compressed yeast
4 tablespoons sugar
4 cups flour

1½ teaspoons salt
1 egg
4 tablespoons fat

Mix as for Yeast Bread, adding the beaten egg after half of the flour has been added. When it has risen to double in bulk smooth the dough on a floured board until it is about ½ inch thick. Cut with a small biscuit cutter into rounds. Then crease these with the dull side of a knife just a little at one side of the middle. Brush the smaller side with melted butter and fold over the wider side. Place far enough apart to prevent them from touching one another. Let rise until double in bulk. Bake at 400 degrees for 15 to 20 minutes.

Yield: Twenty-two 2½-inch rolls.

CHAPTER II

QUICK BREADS

Quick Breads are so called to distinguish them from the breads made of yeast which require at least several hours for their preparation. They can be mixed and baked in a comparatively short time. They are made light by the use of baking powder, soda and sour milk or some other acid ingredient. Some of the most frequently made quick breads are Baking Powder Biscuits and their variations; Bread, Coffee Cake, and Muffins.

* * * *

Biscuits

BAKING POWDER BISCUITS

Temperature, 450 degrees; Time, 14 to 16 minutes

2 cups flour	4 tablespoons fat
4 teaspoons baking powder	¾ cup milk
1 teaspoon salt	

Sift the flour, baking powder and salt together. Cut in the fat until it is evenly mixed with the flour, and add the milk. Stir to mix well. Knead for ½ minute. Roll out about ½ inch thick and cut with a small biscuit cutter. Place the biscuits, 1½ inches apart, on the bottom of a greased baking pan or baking sheet, brush with milk and bake at 450 degrees for 14 to 16 minutes.

Yield: Sixteen to eighteen 1½-inch biscuits.

DUMPLINGS

Temperature, 350 degrees; Time, 15 minutes

1½ cups flour	1 egg
1½ teaspoons baking powder	¾ cup milk
½ teaspoon salt	

Mix as for Baking Powder Biscuits, adding the beaten egg to the milk.

Drop this stiff batter on sauerkraut or meat stews by tablespoonfuls, cover and bake at 350 degrees for 15 minutes.

Yield: 9 large dumplings.

Breads

BOSTON BROWN BREAD

Temperature, 275 degrees; Time, 3 hours

1 tablespoon sugar	2 teaspoons baking
1 cup yellow cornmeal	powder
1 cup white flour	½ teaspoon salt
1 cup whole wheat flour	¾ cup molasses
1 teaspoon soda	1¼ cups milk

Mix the dry ingredients together. Add the molasses and milk. Mix thoroughly and pour into well-greased cylindrical molds. Cover and place them in an uncovered roaster with boiling water surrounding them. Steam at 275 degrees for 3 hours.

Yield: Two loaves, 3½ inches diameter, 4½ inches high.

DATE AND NUT BREAD

Temperature, 350 degrees; Time, 45 minutes

1 egg	2 cups flour
¼ cup sugar	4 teaspoons baking powder
½ cup nut meats	½ teaspoon salt
½ cup dates	1 cup milk

Beat the egg and add the sugar. Add the nut meats, which have been broken, and the dates, which have been washed, stoned and cut into small pieces. Sift the flour, baking powder and salt together and add it alternately with the milk to the first mixture. Then beat to mix well and turn into a greased bread pan. Bake at 350 degrees for 45 minutes.

For Nut Bread use 1 cup of nut meats. For the Date Bread use 1 cup of dates.

Yield: One 4½ x 8½ inch loaf.

Corn Breads

CORN BREAD

Temperature, 400 degrees; Time, 35 to 40 minutes

2 eggs	6 teaspoons baking powder
1½ cups milk	1 teaspoon salt
1½ cups flour	2 tablespoons sugar
1½ cups yellow cornmeal	2 tablespoons butter

Beat the eggs. Add part of the milk to them. Sift the flour once before measuring. Then measure it and add the cornmeal, baking powder, salt and sugar to it. Add the remaining milk and the dry ingredients alternately to the egg and milk mixture. Beat in the melted butter. Pour into a greased pan and bake at 400 degrees for 35 to 40 minutes.

Yield: 1 loaf, 6½ x 10 inches, 2 inches deep.

SPOON CORN BREAD

Temperature, 375 degrees; Time, 50 minutes

1 cup boiling water	½ tablespoon butter
½ cup yellow cornmeal	1 cup milk
½ teaspoon salt	2 eggs

Slowly add the cornmeal to the boiling water, stirring constantly. Cook until thick. Remove from the fire and add the salt and butter. Then add the milk and beaten egg yolks. Lastly fold in the beaten whites and place in a greased shallow baking dish 6½ x 10 x 2 inches. Bake at 375 degrees for 50 minutes.

Yield: 6 servings.

Muffins

PLAIN MUFFINS

Temperature, 400 degrees; Time, 25 minutes

¼ cup butter	4 teaspoons baking powder
¼ cup sugar	½ teaspoon salt
1 egg	1 cup milk
2 cups flour	

Cream the butter and add the sugar gradually, creaming while adding. Then add the well-beaten egg. Sift the flour, baking powder and salt together and add them alternately with the milk to the butter and sugar mixture.

For variation 1 cup of blueberries or other berries may be folded into the muffin mixture. Or, if desired, add ½ cup of chopped dates and ½ cup of chopped nut meats. Bake in greased muffin tins at 400 degrees for 25 minutes.

Yield: 12 muffins, 2½ inches diameter, 1½ inches deep.

BRAN MUFFINS

Temperature, 400 degrees; Time, 25 minutes

1 cup flour	2 tablespoons fat
3 teaspoons baking powder	2 tablespoons brown
½ teaspoon salt	sugar
⅛ teaspoon soda	2 tablespoons molasses
2 cups bran	1 egg
	1 cup milk

Sift the flour, baking powder, salt and soda together. Then add the bran. Cream the fat and add the sugar and molasses. Then add the well-beaten egg. Add the dry ingredients alternately with the milk. Pour into greased muffin tins and bake at 400 degrees for 25 minutes.

Yield: 12 muffins, 2½ inches diameter, 1½ inches deep.

CORNMEAL MUFFINS

Temperature, 400 degrees; Time, 30 minutes

1¼ cups milk	1 cup flour
½ cup cornmeal	3 teaspoons baking powder
1 egg	½ teaspoon salt
1 tablespoon sugar	2 tablespoons fat

Scald the milk and pour ¾ cup of it over the cornmeal. Beat the egg, to which add the cornmeal mixture and sugar. Sift the flour, baking powder and salt together and add these slowly with the ½ cup of milk remaining. Lastly add the melted fat. Bake in greased muffin tins at 400 degrees for 30 minutes.

Yield: 12 muffins, 2½ inches diameter, 1½ inches deep.

GRAHAM MUFFINS

Temperature, 400 degrees; Time, 25 minutes

1 cup Graham flour	¼ cup fat
1 cup white flour	¼ cup sugar
4 teaspoons baking powder	1 egg
¼ teaspoon salt	¾ cup milk

Add the Graham flour to the white flour which has been sifted with the baking powder and salt. Cream the fat and add the sugar and well-beaten egg. Add the dry ingredients alternately with the milk. Bake in greased muffin tins at 400 degrees for 25 minutes.

Yield: 12 muffins, 2½ inches diameter, 1½ inches deep.

OATMEAL MUFFINS

Temperature, 400 degrees; Time, 25 minutes

2 tablespoons fat	2 cups flour
2 tablespoons sugar	3½ teaspoons baking powder
1 egg	¾ teaspoon salt
¼ cup cooked oatmeal	1 cup milk

Mix as for Plain Muffins, adding the cooked oatmeal to the fat, sugar and egg mixture. Three-fourths cup of cooked rice may be used in place of the oatmeal, if desired. Bake in greased muffin tins at 400 degrees for 25 minutes.

Yield: 12 muffins, 2½ inches diameter, 1½ inches deep.

POTATO FLOUR MUFFINS

Temperature, 375 degrees; Time, 20 minutes

3 eggs
2 tablespoons sugar
¾ cup potato flour, or
   potato starch

1 teaspoon baking powder
½ teaspoon salt
4 tablespoons ice water

Separate the eggs and beat the whites until stiff and dry. Beat the yolks until thick and lemon colored, then fold them into the whites. Sift the flour, sugar, baking powder and salt together and fold into the egg mixture. Lastly add the ice water and fold until well mixed. Bake in greased muffin tins at 375 degrees for 20 minutes.

Yield: 12 muffins, 2½ inches diameter, 1½ inches deep.

❦ ❦ ❦ ❦

Popovers

POPOVERS

Temperature, 450 degrees; Time, 25 minutes
then
Temperature, 350 degrees; Time, 15 minutes

2 eggs
1 cup milk
1 cup flour

¼ teaspoon salt
1 tablespoon butter

Beat the eggs and add the milk. Then slowly add the flour and salt which have been sifted together. Beat constantly to prevent lumps. Lastly add the melted butter. Pour into hot greased popover pans and bake at 450 degrees for 25 minutes, then at 350 degrees for 15 minutes.

Yield: 8 popovers, 2½ inches diameter, 3 inches deep.

BUTTERSCOTCH ROLLS

Temperature, 400 degrees; Time, 25 to 30 minutes
or
Temperature, 450 degrees; Time, 15 to 18 minutes

2 cups flour	4 tablespoons fat
4 teaspoons baking powder	⅔ cup milk
1 teaspoon salt	

For Filling

1 tablespoon butter	⅔ cup brown sugar

Mix as for Baking Powder Biscuits. Roll out about ½ inch thick and spread with 1 tablespoon of melted butter mixed with ⅔ cup of brown sugar. Roll as for jelly roll; cut in 1-inch pieces and place close together cut side down in a pan which has 1 tablespoon of butter and ¼ cup of brown sugar in the bottom. These biscuits may be baked in muffin pans if desired, and nuts may be added. Or, ½ teaspoon of cinnamon may be added to the brown sugar which is spread over the dough. Bake at 400 degrees for 25 to 30 minutes. If baked in muffin tins bake at 450 degrees for 15 to 18 minutes.

Yield: 12 to 14 rolls.

SCONES

Temperature, 450 degrees; Time, 12 to 15 minutes

4 tablespoons butter	4 teaspoons baking powder
4 tablespoons sugar	½ teaspoon salt
1 egg	⅝ cup milk
2 cups flour	

Cream the butter and add the sugar and well-beaten egg. Sift the flour, baking powder and salt together and add alternately with the milk. Roll and cut into diamond shapes. Bake on a greased baking sheet at 450 degrees for 12 to 15 minutes.

Yield: 12 to 14 medium size scones.

COFFEE CAKE

Temperature, 400 degrees; Time, 20 minutes

2 cups pastry flour	½ cup sugar
4 teaspoons baking powder	¾ cup milk
½ teaspoon salt	3 tablespoons butter
1 egg	

For Top

2 tablespoons sugar   ½ teaspoon cinnamon

Sift the flour, baking powder and salt together. Combine the ½ cup of sugar, the milk, and the well-beaten egg, and add slowly to the flour mixture. Add the melted butter, and beat until all of the ingredients are thoroughly mixed. Turn the mixture into a greased pan. Mix the 2 tablespoons of sugar and the cinnamon together and sprinkle over the surface of the batter. Bake at 400 degrees for 20 minutes.

If desired, 2 tablespoons of chopped nuts may be added to the sugar and cinnamon mixture, or sliced raw apple may be put on the top and covered with the cinnamon and sugar mixture. If the apple is used it will probably take 5 or 10 minutes longer to bake.

Yield: 1 cake, 9 inches square.

ORANGE BREAD

Temperature, 350 degrees; Time, 55 to 60 minutes

5 tablespoons butter	½ cup orange juice
½ cup sugar	2 cups flour
1 egg	4 teaspoons baking powder
3 tablespoons orange rind	½ teaspoon salt
½ cup water	

Cream the butter and add the sugar gradually, creaming while adding. Then add the beaten egg and the grated rind. Add the water and orange juice alternately with the flour, baking powder and salt which have been sifted together. Mix thoroughly and put in a greased bread pan and let stand 20 minutes before baking. Then bake at 350 degrees for 55 to 60 minutes.

Yield: One 4½ x 8½ inch loaf.

CHAPTER III

CAKES, FROSTINGS AND FILLINGS

In general there are two types of cakes, butter cakes and those of the sponge variety, containing no fat. Loaf, layer or cup cakes can be made from butter cake batter by merely changing the type of pan in which the batter is baked as well as changing the Time and Temperature for baking.

Butter cakes are baked in well-greased pans filled about two-thirds full. Some people prefer to line the bottom of the pan with a piece of clean paper and grease the paper instead of the pan. This insures easy removal of the cake after baking. Some pans have removable bottoms or other devices for easily removing the cake, but if these are lacking the paper in the bottom is a very acceptable substitute. Butter cakes should be removed from the pans as soon as they are taken from the oven, and cooled on a cake cooler. Do not ice cakes until they are cold.

Cup cakes may be made in muffin pans or small paper cases. These cases are inexpensive and are made purposely for baking. Cakes may be left in them until ready to use as they help to keep the cakes fresh.

Sponge cakes are baked in ungreased pans. They should be allowed to remain in the pans inverted on cake racks until cold and then removed by loosening with a spatula.

The recipes given here are merely suggestive of good average cakes which can be made with little trouble. The size of the recipe, i.e. the amount of ingredients used; the size of the pan in which the batter is baked, i.e. the depth of the batter in the pan—both make some difference in the time for baking. Therefore, if other recipes are used than those given here, or if pans of a different size than those in which these recipes were tried are used, some adjustments may have to be made in the length of time for baking.

Materials for Making Cake

Select only the best materials for making cake. This is an important consideration for making a cake of the highest quality, fine texture, and good flavor. Poor eggs, or butter which is even the least bit strong, will be very quickly detected in a cake. It is possible to use other fats than butter. While the texture and fuel value of the cake may be just the same as though butter were used, still there is no other fat which has the butter flavor. There is much difference in flour milled and bought in different parts of the country, so sometimes slight adjustments in the amount of flour or the amount of liquid must be made for the kind of flour in use. *Always sift the flour once before measuring.*

❀　　❀　　❀　　❀

Cakes

ANGEL FOOD CAKE

Temperature, 325 degrees; Time, 1 hour

1¼ cups sugar	1 teaspoon cream of
1 cup specially prepared	tartar
cake flour	1 teaspoon vanilla
1¼ cups egg whites	½ teaspoon almond
¼ teaspoon salt	extract

Sift the sugar and flour before measuring. Sift them four times after measuring. Add the salt to the egg whites and beat until foamy. Sift in the cream of tartar, and beat until stiff but not dry. Add the flavoring and beat until mixed. Add the sugar and flour a little at a time through a sifter to the egg whites. Mix by cutting and folding gently. Turn into an unbuttered 9½-inch tube pan and bake at 325 degrees for 1 hour.

After the cake has been removed from the oven turn it upside down on a cake cooler until it is cold before attempting to remove it from the pan.

BRIDE'S CAKE

Layer
Temperature, 350 degrees; Time, 30 to 35 minutes
Loaf
Temperature, 350 degrees; Time, 50 to 60 minutes
Cup
Temperature, 375 degrees; Time, 18 to 20 minutes

¾ cup butter	½ cup milk
1¼ cups sugar	1 teaspoon vanilla
2 cups specially prepared cake flour	½ teaspoon almond extract
3 teaspoons baking powder	6 egg whites
¼ teaspoon salt	

Cream the butter and add the sugar. Cream these until they are well blended. Sift the flour, baking powder and salt together and add them to the butter and sugar alternately with the milk. Add the flavoring. Beat the egg whites until stiff but not dry, and fold them into the cake batter.

Yield: Two 8-inch layers, one 4½ x 8½ inch loaf, or Fifteen to eighteen cup cakes.

BUTTER SPONGE CAKE

Temperature, 350 degrees; Time, 35 to 40 minutes

1¼ cups specially prepared cake flour	6 eggs
¼ teaspoon salt	1 cup sugar
	1 teaspoon vanilla
	4 tablespoons butter

Sift the flour and salt together three times. Mix the eggs and sugar together and place in the top part of a double boiler. Have the lower part of the boiler filled to ⅓ of its capacity with hot water, but not boiling. Beat until the mixture is almost lukewarm. Remove from the stove and beat for about 7 minutes, or until very fluffy and thick. Fold in the flour mixture, then the vanilla. Add the butter, which should have been melted slowly and not be hot when added to the cake. Mix very carefully and bake at 350 degrees for 35 to 40 minutes.

Yield: 1 shallow loaf 8½ x 12 inches.

CHOCOLATE CAKE

Layer
Temperature, 350 degrees; Time, 35 to 40 minutes

Loaf
Temperature, 350 degrees; Time, 55 to 60 minutes

Cup
Temperature, 375 degrees; Time, 15 to 18 minutes

2¼ cups pastry flour	2 eggs
2 teaspoons baking powder	½ cup sour milk
½ teaspoon soda	½ cup boiling water
¼ teaspoon salt	1½ squares chocolate
½ cup butter	1 teaspoon vanilla
2 cups light brown sugar	

Sift the flour once. Then measure it and add the baking powder, soda and salt. Sift these together 3 times. Cream the butter until light and fluffy. Then add the sugar gradually, creaming thoroughly. Add the well-beaten eggs and beat well so that all of the ingredients are thoroughly mixed. Add the sifted dry ingredients to this mixture alternately with the sour milk. Beat after each addition until smooth. Melt the chocolate over hot water but not boiling. Then stir the ½ cup of boiling water into the melted chocolate and add this to the batter. Add the vanilla.

Bake the layer cake at 350 degrees for 35 to 40 minutes. Loaf cake should be baked at 350 degrees for 55 to 60 minutes.

For cup cakes, muffin pans or paper cases may be used. The length of time for baking cup cakes will depend on the size of the cakes, the average length of time being from 15 to 18 minutes at 375 degrees.

Yield: Two 8-inch layers, one 4½ x 8½ inch loaf, or
Fifteen to eighteen cup cakes.

Sunshine Cake Lives Up to Its Name

FANCY COOKIES ARE SERVED AT INFORMAL TEAS

DELICATE WHITE CAKE

Layer
Temperature, 375 degrees; Time, 30 to 35 minutes
Loaf
Temperature, 350 degrees; Time, 55 to 60 minutes
Cup
Temperature, 375 degrees; Time, 18 to 20 minutes

½ cup butter	¼ teaspoon salt
1 cup sugar	⅔ cup milk
2 cups pastry flour	1 teaspoon vanilla
3½ teaspoons baking powder	4 egg whites

Cream the butter and add the sugar until well blended. Sift the dry ingredients together and add them to the butter and sugar alternately with the milk. Add the flavoring. Beat the egg whites until stiff but not dry, and fold them into the cake batter.

Yield: Two 8-inch layers, one 4½ x 8½ inch loaf, or
Fifteen to eighteen cup cakes.

FEATHER CAKE

Layer

Temperature, 375 degrees; Time, 30 to 35 minutes

Cup

Temperature, 375 degrees; Time, 18 to 20 minutes

3 cups pastry flour	2 cups sugar
4 teaspoons baking powder	4 eggs
¼ teaspoon salt	1 cup milk
½ cup butter	1 teaspoon vanilla

Mix the baking powder and salt with the sifted flour. Cream the butter and add the sugar gradually, creaming while adding. Beat the eggs without separating the whites and yolks. Add to the well-creamed butter and sugar. Sift in the flour mixture a little at a time, alternating with the milk. Add the flavoring and beat long enough to mix thoroughly. Pour into the well-greased pans and bake.

Yield: Two 9-inch layers, three 8-inch layers, or
Twenty-two to twenty-four cup cakes.

29

FRUIT CAKE (Dark)

Temperature, 275 degrees; Time, 3 hours

1 pound citron	1 teaspoon baking powder
1¼ pounds candied apricots	1 teaspoon cinnamon
1½ pounds candied cherries	½ teaspoon cloves
1 pound candied pineapple	1 teaspoon nutmeg
3 pounds seeded raisins	½ pound butter
1 pound currants	½ pound brown sugar
½ pound raw almonds	6 eggs
½ pound flour	1½ cups cider

Thinly slice the citron, apricots and pineapple. Cut the cherries. Wash the raisins and currants and dry them. Blanch and chop the almonds. Mix these ingredients together. Measure the flour after sifting once. Then sift it again with the baking powder and spices added. Combine the fruit and flour mixtures thoroughly. Cream the butter and sugar well. Add the egg yolks and beat thoroughly. Add the cider alternately with the fruit mixture until everything is well mixed. Beat the egg whites until stiff and fold them into the fruit mixture. Line 4 pans 4½ x 8½ inches with unglazed paper. Grease the paper and the sides of the pans, and fill about three-fourths full. Put the pans on a rack in a large pan or roaster. Pour boiling water to a depth of ½ inch or just enough to come to the top of the rack. Cover this large pan and put in the oven at 275 degrees for 2½ hours. At the end of this time remove the cake from it and put the cake back in the oven at 275 degrees and bake for about 30 minutes to dry the cake.

Fruit cake is all the better for having been made well in advance of the time it is to be used. This allows the flavors of the fruits and spices a chance to permeate the cake.

Yield: 10 pounds of cake.

GINGERBREAD

Temperature, 350 degrees; Time, 40 to 45 minutes

½ cup fat
½ cup sugar
2 eggs
2½ cups flour
1½ teaspoons baking powder
½ teaspoon soda

½ teaspoon salt
1 teaspoon ginger
1 teaspoon cinnamon
¼ teaspoon cloves
1 cup molasses
1 cup boiling water

Cream the fat and add the sugar gradually while creaming. Add the beaten eggs, then the previously sifted dry ingredients, alternately with the molasses and water. Beat enough to mix thoroughly and then pour into a well-greased pan and bake at 350 degrees for 40 to 45 minutes.

Yield: One 12 x 7 x 1½ inch gingerbread.

GOLD CAKE

Layer
Temperature, 350 degrees; Time, 30 to 35 minutes
Loaf
Temperature, 325 degrees; Time, 60 to 65 minutes
Cup
Temperature, 375 degrees; Time, 20 to 25 minutes

¾ cup butter
1¼ cups sugar
8 egg yolks
2½ cups specially pre-
    pared cake flour

4 teaspoons baking powder
¼ teaspoon salt
¾ cup milk
1 teaspoon flavoring

Cream the butter until light and fluffy. Add the sugar gradually and continue creaming. Beat the egg yolks until thick and lemon colored, and add them to the butter and sugar mixture. Sift the flour, baking powder and salt together and add them alternately with the milk. Add the flavoring and beat until well mixed.

Yield: Two 9-inch layers, three 8-inch layers, one 8-inch tube loaf, or Twenty-two to twenty-four cup cakes.

31

JELLY ROLL

Temperature, 350 degrees; Time, 25 minutes

1 cup sugar	¼ teaspoon salt
1 cup pastry flour	3 eggs
1 teaspoon baking powder	½ tablespoon milk
1 teaspoon vanilla	1 tablespoon butter

Sift the sugar, flour, baking powder and salt together. Beat the eggs and fold in the sugar and flour mixture gradually with the milk. Add the melted butter and vanilla. Bake in a shallow pan 8 x 12 inches, lined with paper, at 350 degrees for 25 minutes. Remove from the oven and turn onto a hot damp towel. Remove the crusts from the sides and ends of the cake. Spread with jelly or jam which has been beaten to a consistency which will spread easily. Roll, using the damp towel to hold the roll in position. At the end of 15 minutes remove from the towel and roll in powdered sugar.

MARBLE CAKE

Temperature, 350 degrees; Time, 45 minutes

½ cup butter	¼ teaspoon salt
1 cup sugar	½ cup milk
1½ cups pastry flour	1 teaspoon vanilla
1 teaspoon baking powder	4 egg whites

For Chocolate Batter

1 ounce chocolate	1 cup white batter
¼ cup sugar	1½ tablespoons pastry
1 tablespoon milk	flour

Cream the butter until light and fluffy. Add the sugar gradually and continue creaming. Sift the flour, baking powder and salt together and add alternately with the milk to the butter and sugar mixture. Add the flavoring and fold in the stiffly beaten egg whites.

Grate the chocolate, add the sugar and milk to it. Heat and stir until thoroughly blended. To 1 cup of the white batter add the chocolate mixture. Add the 1½ tablespoons of flour. Put a layer of the light batter in a greased pan 6 x 10 inches, then put a layer of dark on top of it. Keep some of the light batter for the top. Bake at 350 degrees for 45 minutes. Remove from the pan and when cold ice with Marble Frosting (see p. 40).

NUT CAKE

Layer
Temperature, 375 degrees; Time, 30 to 35 minutes

Loaf
Temperature, 350 degrees; Time, 55 to 60 minutes

Cup
Temperature, 375 degrees; Time, 18 to 20 minutes

2 cups specially prepared cake flour	1½ cups sugar
2 teaspoons baking powder	1 cup nut meats
¼ teaspoon salt	¾ cup milk
½ cup butter	1 teaspoon vanilla
	4 egg whites

Sift the flour, baking powder and salt together. Cream the butter until very soft and creamy, then slowly add the sugar and continue creaming. Add about 2 tablespoons of the flour mixture to the broken nut meats. Then add the remaining flour mixture alternately with the milk to the butter and sugar. Add the nuts and flavoring. Beat the egg whites until stiff, but not dry and fold into the cake batter.

Yield: Two 8-inch layers, one 4½ x 8½ inch loaf, or
Fifteen to eighteen cup cakes.

ORANGE GOLD CAKE

Layer
Temperature, 375 degrees; Time, 30 to 35 minutes
Loaf
Temperature, 350 degrees; Time, 55 to 60 minutes
Cup
Temperature, 375 degrees; Time, 18 to 20 minutes

2 cups pastry flour
3½ teaspoons baking powder
¼ teaspoon salt
½ cup butter
1 cup sugar

4 egg yolks
⅔ cup milk
1 tablespoon orange juice
1 teaspoon orange rind

Sift the flour, baking powder and salt together. Cream the butter very thoroughly and add the sugar gradually, creaming until well dissolved. Add the well-beaten egg yolks. Beat vigorously and then add the flour mixture alternately with the milk. Add the flavoring and beat until well mixed.

Yield: Two 8-inch layers, one 4½ x 8½ inch loaf, or Fifteen to eighteen cup cakes.

PLAIN CAKE

Layer
Temperature, 375 degrees; Time, 30 to 35 minutes
Loaf
Temperature, 350 degrees; Time, 55 to 60 minutes
Cup
Temperature, 375 degrees; Time, 18 to 20 minutes

2 cups pastry flour
3 teaspoons baking powder
¼ teaspoon salt
½ cup butter

1 cup sugar
2 eggs
¾ cup milk
1 teaspoon vanilla

Mix the baking powder and salt with the sifted flour. Cream the butter until the consistency is even and soft enough to beat easily. Then add the sugar gradually, creaming while adding. Beat the eggs without separating them, and add to the well-creamed butter and sugar. Sift in the flour mixture a little at a time, alternating with the milk. Add the flavoring and beat the batter vigorously only long enough to mix thoroughly. Pour into the well-greased cake pans and bake.

Yield: Two 8-inch layers, one 4½ x 8½ inch loaf, or Fifteen to eighteen cup cakes.

PLAIN CUP CAKES

Temperature, 375 degrees; Time, 18 to 20 minutes

½ cup butter	1¾ cups pastry flour
1 cup sugar	2 teaspoons baking powder
3 eggs	¼ teaspoon salt
½ cup milk	1 teaspoon vanilla

Cream the butter and add the sugar gradually, stirring until they are well mixed. Stir in the beaten eggs. Add the milk alternately with the flour, which has been sifted before measuring and sifted again with the baking powder and salt. When the batter is smooth, add the vanilla. Bake at 375 degrees for 18 to 20 minutes.

Yield: Fifteen 2½-inch cup cakes.

POUND CAKE

Temperature, 325 degrees; Time, 2 hours

1 pound butter	1 orange rind, grated
1 pound sugar	1 pound specially prepared
9 eggs	cake flour

Cream the butter until very soft and smooth. Add the sugar gradually, beating all the time. A very thorough blending of the butter and sugar is essential for a fine texture. Add the unbeaten eggs, one at a time, beating well after each addition. Next add the grated orange rind. Then add the flour and beat until well mixed and smooth. Turn into a greased 9½-inch tube pan and bake at 325 degrees for 2 hours.

One half this recipe may be baked in a loaf pan 4½ x 8½ inches, at 325 degrees for 1½ hours.

SPICE CAKE

Layer
Temperature, 375 degrees; Time, 30 to 35 minutes

Loaf
Temperature, 350 degrees; Time, 55 to 60 minutes

Cup
Temperature, 375 degrees; Time, 18 to 20 minutes

2 cups pastry flour
½ teaspoon cinnamon
½ teaspoon cloves
½ teaspoon ginger
¼ teaspoon salt

3½ teaspoons baking powder
½ cup butter
1 cup sugar
2 eggs
½ cup milk

Sift the flour, spices, salt and baking powder together. Cream the butter and sugar, and add the well-beaten eggs. Beat until light and fluffy. Add the milk alternately with the flour mixture.

Yield: Two 8-inch layers, one 4½ x 8½ inch loaf, or Fifteen to eighteen cup cakes.

SPONGE CAKE

Layer
Temperature, 325 degrees; Time, 40 minutes

Loaf
Temperature, 325 degrees; Time, 1 hour

Cup
Temperature, 350 degrees; Time, 15 to 18 minutes

6 eggs
½ teaspoon salt
½ teaspoon cream of tartar

½ lemon rind
1 cup sugar
1 cup pastry flour

Separate the eggs and add the salt to the egg whites. Beat until foamy. Then add the cream of tartar and beat until stiff but not dry. Beat in the grated lemon rind and then fold in the egg yolks which have been beaten until thick and lemon colored. Carefully fold in the sugar and flour which have been sifted together several times.

Yield: Two 9-inch layers, one 9½-inch tube loaf, or Twenty-two to twenty-four cup cakes.

SPONGE LOAF CAKE

Temperature, 350 degrees; Time, 45 to 50 minutes

1 cup pastry flour	3 tablespoons cold water
1 cup sugar	1 teaspoon vanilla
4 eggs	

Measure the flour after sifting once. Then sift it again with the sugar 5 times. Separate the eggs and beat the yolks until they are thick and lemon colored. Add the water and continue beating. Add the vanilla and then fold in the flour and sugar. Lastly fold in the stiffly beaten egg whites. Bake in an ungreased 7-inch tube pan at 350 degrees for 45 to 50 minutes.

Yield: One 7-inch tube loaf cake.

SUNSHINE CAKE

Temperature, 325 degrees; Time, 1 hour

8 egg whites, 1 cup	6 egg yolks, ⅝ cup
¼ teaspoon salt	½ orange rind
1 teaspoon cream of tartar	1¼ cups specially pre-
1⅓ cups sugar	pared cake flour

Beat the egg whites with the salt until they are foamy. Add the cream of tartar and beat until stiff. Fold in the sugar. Beat the egg yolks until thick and lemon colored. Fold about ⅛ of the egg white mixture into the yolks. Blend well using a folding motion, then add this to the remaining egg whites. Add the grated orange rind and fold in the flour, sifted once before and several times after measuring. Bake in an ungreased 9½-inch tube pan at 325 degrees for 1 hour.

Yield: One 9½-inch tube loaf cake.

Frostings and Fillings

BOILED FROSTING

2 cups sugar
¼ cup white corn
   syrup

6 tablespoons water
2 egg whites
1 teaspoon vanilla

Cook the sugar, syrup and water together over a surface burner until it reaches a temperature of 240 degrees Fahrenheit, or forms a soft ball in cold water. Turn off the fire and let the syrup stand over the warm burner while quickly beating the egg whites with a rotary egg beater. Pour the syrup slowly over the beaten egg whites, beating with a spoon while adding. Add the vanilla and beat until almost cold. This mixture should hold its shape when spread on a cake.

Put any left-over frosting in a jar; cover tightly, and keep in the refrigerator. It will keep fresh for at least a week. Then, if necessary, add a small amount of hot water and beat until it is a good consistency to spread.

BUTTER CREAM FROSTING

1 tablespoon butter
1½ tablespoons cream
⅛ teaspoon salt

½ teaspoon vanilla
¾ cup confectioners'
   sugar

Melt the butter and add the cream. Then add the salt, vanilla and sugar. Stir until the ingredients are well mixed.

Coffee or lemon juice may be used instead of the cream. When these materials are used, the vanilla should be omitted.

CHOCOLATE FILLING

1 ounce chocolate
1 cup milk
⅜ cup sugar
1 tablespoon cornstarch

2 tablespoons flour
¼ teaspoon salt
1 tablespoon butter
1 teaspoon vanilla

Cut the chocolate into pieces and melt it in the top part of a double boiler over hot water. Then add the milk to this and continue heating. Mix the sugar, cornstarch, flour and salt. Then pour a portion of the hot milk mixture into it and stir until the ingredients are blended. Pour this back into the remainder of the milk mixture in the top of the double boiler. Stir and cook until the milk is thickened. Continue cooking for 15 minutes longer, stirring occasionally. Remove from the fire. Add the butter and vanilla, and stir until the butter is melted. Set aside to cool, then spread between the layers of any plain cake.

CHOCOLATE FROSTING

Follow the directions given for Boiled Frosting on p. 38, adding 2 ounces of melted chocolate after the frosting is cool enough to hold its shape. The chocolate should be warmed until soft but not thin.

COCOANUT FROSTING

2 cups sugar
6 tablespoons water
¼ cup white corn syrup
2 egg whites

1 teaspoon vanilla
1 cup moist cocoanut or
2 cups grated fresh
cocoanut

Put the sugar, water and syrup in a sauce pan and cook to 240 degrees Fahrenheit or until it forms a soft ball in cold water. Turn off the flame and let the syrup stand over the burner while quickly beating the egg whites. Pour the syrup over the egg whites, beating constantly. Then add the vanilla. Beat until cool enough to hold its shape. Spread on the cake and sprinkle cocoanut generously on frosting.

CUSTARD FILLING

1 pint milk	1 egg
¼ cup flour	¼ teaspoon salt
1 tablespoon cornstarch	1 teaspoon vanilla
¾ cup sugar	or 1 tablespoon
1 tablespoon butter	cooking sherry

Scald the milk in the top of a double boiler. Mix the flour, cornstarch and sugar in a bowl. Stir these materials and gradually pour the hot milk over them. When well mixed, return to the double boiler. Stir and cook until the mixture thickens. Then cover and continue cooking for 15 minutes longer. Add the butter. Beat the egg and add the salt to it. Add this gradually to the milk mixture, stirring vigorously while combining. Stir and cook until the egg is thickened. Cool, and stir in the flavoring.

A more delicate texture and finer flavor may be produced by folding ¼ pint of cream, which has been whipped, into the cooled custard. This recipe makes a nice dessert. For six servings double the recipe.

MARBLE FROSTING

½ pound marshmallows   Chocolate frosting

Cut the marshmallows into quarters or halves and place with the cut surface on the top of the cake while it is still warm. Pour the chocolate frosting (see p. 39) over the marshmallows.

MOCHA FROSTING

⅓ cup butter	2 tablespoons cold
1½ cups confectioners' sugar	coffee

Cream the butter and add the sugar and coffee. The frosting will be ready to spread on a cake when it holds its shape well.

ORANGE FILLING

½ cup sugar
¼ cup flour
½ cup water
1 tablespoon cornstarch
½ orange rind

¼ cup orange juice
½ tablespoon lemon juice
1 egg
1 tablespoon butter

In the top part of a double boiler mix the sugar, flour, water and cornstarch. Add the grated orange rind and cook this mixture over hot water until it thickens, stirring constantly. Let it cook for 15 minutes more, stirring occasionally. Then add the orange and lemon juice, the beaten egg, and the butter. Stir vigorously and cook for 3 minutes. Remove the top part of the double boiler from the lower part, and set aside to cool.

ORANGE FROSTING

Orange Frosting may be made by using the recipe for Butter Cream Frosting (p. 38), substituting 1 tablespoon of orange juice and ½ tablespoon of lemon juice for the cream. Or, it may also be made by adding 2 tablespoons of orange juice to the Boiled Frosting recipe (p. 38), instead of the vanilla.

CHAPTER IV

COOKIES AND SMALL CAKES

Cookies are often baked on baking sheets. If used they should not cover the entire surface of the grate. At least 2 inches should be allowed between the wall of the oven and the edge of the cooky sheet. Only 1 sheet should be used in the oven at a time. Otherwise the circulation of heat is not properly distributed and uneven baking may result. Inverted cake pans may also be used. Always remove cookies from the pans while hot. Let cool on a cake cooler before putting in the cooky jar.

Bake small cakes in muffin tins or in paper cases which are made expressly for the purpose. The paper cases will help to keep the cakes fresh and make fewer pans to wash.

PLAIN COOKIES

Temperature, 375 degrees; Time, 10 to 15 minutes

1 cup butter
1½ cups sugar
2 eggs
4 cups pastry flour
3 teaspoons baking powder
⅛ teaspoon soda
1 teaspoon salt
2 teaspoons nutmeg
¼ cup sour milk or cream

Cream the butter and add the sugar gradually, creaming while adding. Add the beaten eggs and beat the mixture until the ingredients are blended. Sift the flour once before measuring. Then add the baking powder, soda, salt and nutmeg to it. Sift together and add alternately with the milk or cream to the egg mixture. Place in the refrigerator or other cool place over night to make it easier to roll out. Sprinkle a little flour over a pastry board. Roll out into a thin sheet a small portion of the chilled dough at a time. Cut it into rounds or other shapes with a cooky cutter. If desired, sugar may be sprinkled over the dough after it is rolled out. Place the cookies on a greased baking sheet and bake at 375 degrees for 10 to 15 minutes.

Yield: 6 dozen 2½-inch cookies.

BAKED FUDGE

Temperature, 350 degrees; Time, 40 to 45 minutes

2 ounces chocolate
¼ cup milk
2 eggs
1 cup sugar
½ cup pastry flour

½ teaspoon salt
1 teaspoon vanilla
1 cup nut meats
⅓ cup butter

Cut the chocolate into pieces and put it and the milk in a small sauce pan. Stir and cook over a low flame until a smooth thick paste is formed. Beat the eggs and then add the sugar. Stir until it is dissolved in the eggs. Cool the chocolate paste, then add it to the egg and sugar mixture. Measure the flour after sifting once. Add the salt and sift again into the above mixture. Then add the vanilla and chopped nut meats. Stir well. Melt the butter and add to the other ingredients. Beat well and turn into a greased pan 9 x 9 inches. Bake at 350 degrees for 40 to 45 minutes. Cool and cut into squares.

Yield: 16 squares.

BUTTERSCOTCH COOKIES

Temperature, 375 degrees; Time, 12 to 15 minutes

2 eggs
2 cups brown sugar
¾ cup butter
3½ cups pastry flour

2 tablespoons baking powder
½ teaspoon salt
1 teaspoon vanilla
1 cup walnut meats

Beat the eggs and add the sugar until it is well dissolved. Melt the butter and add it to the egg and sugar mixture. Sift the flour before measuring, then add the baking powder and salt and sift slowly into the first mixture. Add the vanilla and finely chopped nut meats. Put this through a cooky press and bake, or shape into a cylinder or rectangle and let stand in the refrigerator overnight. Cut the dough into thin slices. Place on a greased baking sheet and bake at 375 degrees for 12 to 15 minutes.

Yield: 4 dozen 2½-inch cookies.

CHOCOLATE COCOANUT CAKES

Temperature, 350 degrees; Time, 15 minutes

2 ounces chocolate	1 tablespoon flour
¼ cup water	¼ teaspoon salt
¾ cup sugar	2 teaspoons vanilla
½ pound moist cocoanut	3 egg whites

Grate the chocolate, add the water. Stir and cook over a low flame until a thick smooth paste is formed. Remove from the fire and add the sugar and cocoanut. Then fold in the flour, salt and vanilla. Beat the egg whites until they are stiff and fold them into the other ingredients. Drop by teaspoonfuls on the bottom of a greased pan or baking sheet and bake at 350 degrees for 15 minutes.

Yield: 2 to 2½ dozen 1½-inch cakes.

COCOANUT DAINTIES

Temperature, 375 degrees; Time, 10 to 12 minutes

2 egg whites	½ cup white corn syrup
½ cup sugar	4 cups moist cocoanut
½ cup flour	

Beat the egg whites until stiff. Add the sugar to them gradually, folding it in so they will retain their fluffiness. Continue this folding while adding the flour, corn syrup and cocoanut. Drop by teaspoonfuls on the bottom of a well-greased pan or baking sheet. Bake at 375 degrees for 10 to 12 minutes.

Yield: 2 dozen 1½-inch cakes.

DATE BARS

Temperature, 350 degrees; Time, 30 minutes

1 cup pastry flour	1 cup nut meats
1 teaspoon baking powder	3 eggs
¼ teaspoon salt	1 cup sugar
1 10-ounce package dates	3 tablespoons water

Measure and sift the baking powder and salt with the flour which has been measured after sifting once. Add the dates which have been washed, stoned and cut in small pieces, and the nuts which have been broken. Mix thoroughly and then beat the eggs until they are light. Add the sugar gradually. Stir in the dry ingredients with the nuts and dates. Then add the water and place this mixture in 2 shallow 6 x 10-inch pans which have been well greased. Put only a thin layer of batter over the bottom of the pans. Bake at 350 degrees for 30 minutes. Remove from the oven, cut into strips about 4 inches long by 1 inch wide and while still warm roll each strip in confectioners' sugar.

Yield: 2 to 2½ dozen bars.

DROP CAKES

Temperature, 375 degrees; Time, 12 to 15 minutes

½ cup butter	2 cups pastry flour
1 cup sugar	3½ teaspoons baking powder
2 eggs	¼ teaspoon salt
1½ tablespoons milk	1 teaspoon vanilla

Cream the butter and add the sugar gradually, creaming while adding. Add the well-beaten eggs, then add the milk alternately with the dry ingredients which have been sifted together. Add the vanilla and mix well. Drop by teaspoonfuls on a greased pan and bake at 375 degrees for 12 to 15 minutes.

For Chocolate Drop Cakes use the same recipe and method, adding 2 ounces of melted chocolate to the butter and egg mixture.

Yield: 3 dozen cakes.

45

GINGER WAFERS

Temperature, 375 degrees; Time, 6 to 8 minutes

1 cup molasses	¾ teaspoon cloves
½ cup butter	¾ teaspoon cinnamon
½ cup brown sugar	¼ teaspoon nutmeg
3¾ cups pastry flour	½ teaspoon allspice
¾ teaspoon ginger	¾ teaspoon soda

Heat the molasses and butter. Stir until they are well mixed. Add the sugar. Then sift the flour before measuring and add the remaining ingredients and sift again. Beat them into the first mixture. Put in the refrigerator over night. The next day roll very thin, on a slightly floured board, and cut with a cooky cutter. Bake at 375 degrees for 6 to 8 minutes.

Yield: 6 dozen 2½-inch cookies.

HONEY DROP CAKES

Temperature, 375 degrees; Time, 15 minutes

½ cup butter	1 cup honey
½ cup sugar	3½ cups pastry flour
2 eggs	1 teaspoon soda
1 lemon rind	¼ teaspoon salt
3 tablespoons lemon juice	1 cup nut meats

Cream the butter and add the sugar, creaming while adding. Then beat in the well-beaten eggs. Add the lemon rind, grated, and the lemon juice and honey. Add the flour which has been sifted before measuring and the soda and salt which have then been sifted together with the flour. Stir in the chopped nut meats. Mix thoroughly and drop by teaspoonfuls on a greased baking sheet or pan about 2 inches apart. Bake at 375 degrees for 15 minutes.

Yield: 5½ dozen cakes.

LADY FINGERS

Temperature, 350 degrees; Time, 10 minutes

3 egg whites
⅛ teaspoon salt
⅓ cup powder   sugar

2 egg yolks
¼ teaspoon vanilla
⅓ cup pastry flour

Add the salt to t   egg whites and beat them until they are stiff and dry. Fold in the sugar gradually. Then add the yolks, beaten until they are thick and lemon colored. Add the flavoring. Cut and fold in the flour which has been measured after sifting once. Shape about 4½ inches long and ¾ inch wide on the bottom of a pan covered with unbuttered paper. Lady Finger pans may be used for baking, or shaping can be facilitated by the use of a pastry bag and tube. Bake at 350 degrees for 10 minutes.

Yield: 2½ dozen cakes.

NUT MERINGUES

Temperature, 275 degrees; Time, 35 to 40 minutes

4 egg whites
⅛ teaspoon salt
1 cup sugar

1 teaspoon vanilla
1 cup nut meats

Add the salt to the egg whites and beat the mixture until stiff. Then add the sugar and vanilla, folding these ingredients together. Continue mixing only long enough to blend the sugar with the other ingredients. Stir in the chopped nut meats. Drop this mixture by teaspoonfuls on a paper covered baking sheet or pan. Bake at 275 degrees for 35 to 40 minutes.

One cup of washed, stoned and cut dates may be added if desired.

Yield: 3½ dozen meringues.

OATMEAL SPICE CAKES

Temperature, 375 degrees; Time, 12 to 15 minutes

1 egg	½ teaspoon nutmeg
½ cup sugar	⅛ teaspoon soda
2 tablespoons milk	½ teaspoon baking powder
1 cup dry rolled oats	½ cup butter
1 cup pastry flour	½ cup nut meats
1 teaspoon cinnamon	½ cup raisins

Beat the egg, add the sugar and milk. Mix well, then add the rolled oats. Mix the spices, soda and baking powder with the flour which has been sifted before measuring. Sift them into the first mixture. Melt the butter and add. Add the chopped nut meats and raisins and stir until well mixed. Drop by teaspoonfuls on a greased baking sheet or pan and bake at 375 degrees for 12 to 15 minutes.

Yield: 2½ dozen cakes.

PEANUT MACAROONS

Temperature, 325 degrees; Time, 20 minutes

2 eggs	2 tablespoons flour
⅞ cup sugar	¼ teaspoon salt
2¾ cups roasted peanut meats	1 teaspoon vanilla

Beat the eggs, add the sugar and mix well. Put the peanuts through a food chopper, using the coarse wheel, without removing their dark brittle covering. Mix the flour, salt and peanuts and add them to the egg mixture. Then add the vanilla and mix well. Drop by teaspoonfuls onto buttered pans. Bake at 325 degrees for 20 minutes. Remove from the pans at once to a cake cooler.

Yield: 3 dozen macaroons.

PECAN SQUARES

Temperature, 350 degrees; Time, 25 minutes

2 eggs	½ cup pastry flour
1 cup brown sugar	⅓ cup butter
½ cup pecan meats	1 teaspoon vanilla

Beat the eggs and add the sugar. Then add the broken pecan meats, sifted flour, and melted butter. Lastly add the vanilla. Pour into a 9-inch square pan and bake at 350 degrees for 25 minutes. When cool cut into squares.

Yield: 16 squares.

ROCKS

Temperature, 350 degrees; Time, 18 minutes

1 cup butter	1 teaspoon cinnamon
1½ cups brown sugar	½ teaspoon salt
3 eggs	1 cup raisins
3¼ cups pastry flour	1 cup walnut meats
1 teaspoon soda	1½ tablespoons water

Cream the butter and add the sugar gradually. Then add the well-beaten eggs. Sift the soda, cinnamon and salt with the flour which has been measured after sifting once. Mix part of the flour mixture to the chopped raisins and chopped nut meats. Add to the egg and sugar mixture. Add the water and then the remaining flour mixture. Drop by teaspoonfuls on well-greased baking pans. Bake at 350 degrees for 18 minutes.

Yield: 3½ dozen cakes.

VANILLA WAFERS

Temperature, 375 degrees; Time, 10 to 12 minutes

½ cup butter	2⅔ cups pastry flour
1½ cups sugar	1 teaspoon salt
2 eggs	2 teaspoons baking powder
4 tablespoons milk	2 teaspoons vanilla

Cream the butter and add the sugar, creaming while adding. Then add the well-beaten eggs. Add the milk and the dry ingredients which have been sifted together. Lastly add the vanilla. Drop by teaspoonfuls on a well-greased baking sheet or put through a cooky press. Bake at 375 degrees for 10 to 12 minutes.

Yield: 5 dozen cookies.

CHAPTER V

DESSERTS

Fruit Desserts

BAKED APPLES

Temperature, 400 degrees; Time, 35 to 40 minutes

6 baking apples
6 tablespoons sugar
¾ teaspoon cinnamon

½ tablespoon flour
1½ teaspoons butter
½ cup water

Wash and core the apples. Peel a strip around the middle and place in a baking dish. Mix the sugar, cinnamon and flour together and pour into the cavity of each apple. Put ¼ teaspoon of butter on each and pour the ½ cup of water in the bottom of the baking dish. Bake at 400 degrees for 35 to 40 minutes.

For a pleasing variation, fill the centers with cranberry or other tart jelly. The apples will then make a nice accompaniment to a meat course.

Yield: 6 servings.

SCALLOPED APPLES

Temperature, 400 degrees; Time, 30 minutes

6 medium apples
¼ teaspoon cinnamon
¼ teaspoon salt
1 tablespoon lemon juice

¼ cup water
¾ cup brown sugar
¼ cup flour
⅓ cup butter

Pare, core and slice the apples. Place in a buttered casserole and add the cinnamon, salt, lemon juice and water. Work the sugar, flour and butter together until crumblike in consistency. Spread this over the apples and bake at 400 degrees for 30 minutes.

Yield: 6 servings.

APPLE DUMPLINGS

Temperature, 425 degrees; Time, 35 to 40 minutes

1½ cups flour	6 apples
½ teaspoon salt	6 tablespoons sugar
½ cup fat	¾ teaspoon cinnamon
4½ tablespoons water	¾ teaspoon butter

For Syrup

1 cup water	¼ cup butter
½ cup sugar	

Make a paste of the flour, salt, fat and water according to the directions for Plain Pastry on p. 94. Roll out and cut into 6-inch squares. Place a pared and cored apple on each square. Add 1 tablespoon of sugar, ⅛ teaspoon of cinnamon, and ⅛ teaspoon of butter to each apple. Fold the dough around the apples. Prick with a fork and place in a baking dish. Heat the water, sugar and butter together until the sugar and butter are melted. Then pour this syrup around the dumplings. Bake at 425 degrees for 35 to 40 minutes.

Yield: 6 servings.

PEACH COBBLER

Temperature, 450 degrees; Time, 30 minutes

12 halves of peaches	2 teaspoons baking powder
⅓ cup sugar	2 tablespoons fat
2 tablespoons water	⅜ cup milk
1 cup pastry flour	

Place the halves of either fresh or canned peaches in the bottom of a glass baking dish and add the sugar and water. Syrup from the canned peaches may be substituted for the water if desired. Mix and sift the dry ingredients. Cut in the fat and add the milk. Mix lightly and spread the dough over the peaches in a buttered baking dish. Bake at 450 degrees for 30 minutes. Other fruits or berries may be used instead of the peaches.

Yield: 6 servings.

PEACH ROLY POLY

Temperature, 400 degrees; Time, 45 minutes

2 cups pastry flour	4 tablespoons fat
4 teaspoons baking powder	2/3 cup milk
1/2 teaspoon salt	

For Filling

1 1/2 cups peaches	2 tablespoons butter
1/3 cup sugar	1 cup boiling water

Sift the dry ingredients together. Cut in the fat and add the milk to make a soft dough that can be easily handled. Roll out 1/2 inch thick on a lightly floured board. Spread with the sliced peaches, either fresh or canned, and sprinkle with sugar. Roll and place in a buttered baking dish. Spread with the butter. Add the boiling water and bake at 400 degrees for 45 minutes.

Other fillings may be used. The following one is pleasing:

1 cup cranberries	1/2 cup sugar
1/2 cup walnut meats	2 tablespoons butter
1/2 cup raisins	1 cup boiling water

Wash the cranberries and add the chopped nut meats, and raisins and sugar. Mix well and spread this mixture over the dough in place of the peaches. Proceed according to the above directions.

Yield: 8 servings.

STRAWBERRY SHORTCAKE

Temperature, 450 degrees; Time, 15 to 18 minutes

2 cups pastry flour	6 tablespoons fat
4 teaspoons baking powder	3/4 cup milk
1/2 teaspoon salt	

Sift the flour, baking powder and salt together and work the fat in with a fork. Add the milk and roll out to about 3/4 inch thickness on a floured board. Cut with a 2 1/2-inch biscuit cutter and place on a greased baking pan. Brush over the tops of the biscuits with milk and bake at 450 degrees for 15 to 18 minutes.

Wash and hull 1½ quarts berries. Save out a few of the best ones and crush the rest. Sweeten to suit the taste with from ½ to ¾ cup of sugar. Split each biscuit and butter while hot. Cover with the crushed strawberries which have been allowed to stand in the sugar. Put a few whole berries on top for a garnish and serve with whipped or plain cream.

Yield: 6 servings.

* * * *

Cream Puffs and Éclairs

CREAM PUFFS

Small

Temperature, 450 degrees; Time, 15 minutes

then

Temperature, 325 degrees; Time, 20 minutes

Large

Temperature, 450 degrees; Time, 20 minutes

then

Temperature, 325 degrees; Time, 20 minutes

1 cup water	¼ teaspoon salt
½ cup butter	4 eggs
1 cup pastry flour	

Put the water and butter in a sauce pan and heat until the water boils. Pour the flour and salt into the hot mixture and beat thoroughly. Stir and cook over a low flame until the mixture forms a stiff ball. Remove from the fire and add the unbeaten eggs, one at a time, beating thoroughly after each egg is added. Drop by teaspoonfuls, or tablespoonfuls for larger puffs, on a greased baking sheet. If small puffs are desired bake at 450 degrees for 15 minutes, then 325 degrees for 20 minutes. For larger puffs bake at 450 degrees for 20 minutes, then 325 degrees for 20 minutes. Fill with Custard Filling (see page 40) or sweetened whipped cream.

Yield: 3 dozen tiny puffs, or
10 large puffs.

CHOCOLATE ÉCLAIRS

Temperature, 450 degrees; Time, 15 minutes
then
Temperature, 325 degrees; Time, 20 minutes

Use the recipe for Cream Puff Shells (see page 53). Shape with a spoon, or put through a pastry tube, in pieces 3 inches long and 1 inch wide. Bake at 450 degrees for 15 minutes, then at 325 degrees for 20 minutes.

When cool fill with Chocolate Filling (see page 38). It will be necessary to use double that recipe to fill all of the éclairs.

Yield: 15 éclairs.

* * * *

Custards

CARAMEL CUSTARD

Temperature, 350 degrees; Time, 40 minutes

¾ cup sugar
4 cups milk
6 eggs

¼ teaspoon salt
1 teaspoon vanilla

Heat the dry sugar in a small pan over a low flame, stirring until it melts and becomes a light amber color. Add 2 tablespoons of boiling water and pour it slowly into the milk which has been scalded. Beat the eggs, add the salt and vanilla and slowly pour the milk mixture on them. Bake at 350 degrees for 40 minutes in a casserole set in a pan of hot water. If the custard is done a silver knife should be clean when withdrawn from the center of it.

Yield: 8 servings.

CUP CUSTARD

Temperature, 350 degrees; Time, 30 to 35 minutes

3 eggs   3 cups milk
⅓ cup sugar   ¾ teaspoon vanilla
¼ teaspoon salt

Beat the eggs and add the other ingredients. Mix thoroughly. Strain the mixture and pour into 6 custard cups of ½ cup or 4 ounce capacity. Place the cups in a pan and pour boiling water in it to a depth of 1 inch. Bake uncovered at 350 degrees for 30 to 35 minutes. If the custard is done a silver knife should be clean when withdrawn from the center of it.

Yield: 6 servings.

GINGERBREAD CUSTARD

Temperature, 350 degrees; Time, 1 hour

2 egg yolks   1 pint milk
¼ cup sugar   1 cup gingerbread crumbs

Beat the egg yolks, then add the sugar and scalded milk. Pour them over the stale gingerbread crumbs which have been placed in a buttered baking dish. Place the dish in a pan of hot water and bake at 350 degrees for 1 hour.

A meringue may be made according to the directions given on p. 63 and spread on the custard 15 minutes before removing it from the oven. The pudding is done when a clean silver knife is uncoated upon removal from the center of the custard.

Yield: 5 servings.

Puddings

All of these puddings may be served plain or with whipped cream. A pudding sauce (see page 111) may be selected if desired.

APRICOT AND RICE PUDDING

Temperature, 275 degrees; Time, 3 hours*

1 cup rice	2 tablespoons butter
½ pound dried apricots	4 cups cold water
½ cup sugar	¼ teaspoon salt

Wash the rice and put it in a buttered casserole. Add the apricots washed and cut in small pieces, together with the rest of the ingredients. Cover and bake at 275 degrees for 3 hours.

One cup of dates, stoned and cut into pieces, may be substituted for the dried apricots.

Yield: 6 servings.

BREAD PUDDING

Temperature, 350 degrees; Time, 1¼ hours

1 quart milk	¼ teaspoon salt
2 cups bread cubes	1 teaspoon vanilla
3 eggs	3 tablespoons butter
½ cup sugar	

Scald the milk and pour it over the bread which has been cut into ½-inch cubes. Let stand 10 minutes. Beat the eggs slightly. Add the sugar, salt and vanilla to them. Put into a buttered baking dish and add the milk and bread cubes. Add the melted butter and stir to mix well. Place the dish in a shallow pan of boiling water. Bake at 350 degrees for 1¼ hours.

For Chocolate Bread Pudding add 2 ounces of melted chocolate before the melted butter is put in. Bake at 350 degrees for 1¼ hours.

Yield: 6 servings.

---

* This time and temperature is suitable for oven meals.

CHERRY PUDDING

Temperature, 400 degrees; Time, 1 hour

or

Temperature, 275 degrees; Time, 3 hours*

1½ cups pastry flour	2 cups cherries
2 teaspoons baking powder	1 egg
½ teaspoon salt	½ cup milk
¼ cup sugar	3 tablespoons butter

Sift together the dry ingredients. Then add the cherries which have been washed and stoned, if fresh, or well drained from the liquid, if canned. Beat the egg and add to the milk. Add this slowly to the dry ingredients. Add the melted butter and mix well. Pour into buttered molds and place in the oven in a steamer with about 1½ inches of boiling water in it. Cover the steamer but do not cover the molds. Let cook at either of the above temperatures for the required length of time.

Yield: 6 servings.

CHOCOLATE PUDDING

Temperature, 400 degrees; Time, 1 hour

or

Temperature, 275 degrees; Time, 3 hours*

2 cups pastry flour	1 cup sugar
3 teaspoons baking powder	1 cup milk
¼ teaspoon salt	2 ounces chocolate
1 egg	

Sift the flour, baking powder and salt together. Add the beaten egg and sugar. Then add the milk and chocolate which has been melted over hot water. Pour into 2 well-greased molds until they are about two-thirds full. Do not cover the molds. Place them in a large pan containing 1½ inches of boiling water and cover this.

This pudding may be made in individual molds. These individual puddings will be done in a half hour if steamed at 400 degrees. If the lower temperature is selected, because a whole meal is being prepared in the oven, the pudding should be allowed to steam the full length of time.

Yield: 8 servings.

---

* This time and temperature is suitable for oven meals.

COCOANUT AND DATE BREAD PUDDING

Temperature, 350 degrees; Time, 1½ hours

3 cups stale bread cubes
½ cup shredded cocoanut
⅔ cup dates
2 eggs

¼ cup sugar
2 cups milk
½ teaspoon salt
1 teaspoon vanilla

Put the stale bread cubes, cocoanut and dates in a buttered casserole. Beat the eggs, add the sugar, then the milk, salt and vanilla. Pour this over the bread mixture and place in the oven at 350 degrees for 1½ hours. Serve with cream.

Yield: 6 servings.

COTTAGE PUDDING

Temperature, 375 degrees; Time, 40 to 45 minutes

Prepare any inexpensive plain cake. Bake in a rectangular pan 6½ x 10 inches at 375 degrees for 40 to 45 minutes. Serve hot with any one of the sweet Dessert Sauces.

CRANBERRY PUDDING

Temperature, 400 degrees; Time, 1 hour

1½ cups pastry flour
2 teaspoons baking powder
½ teaspoon salt
¼ cup sugar

2 cups cranberries
1 egg
½ cup milk
3 tablespoons butter

Sift together the flour, baking powder, salt and sugar. Then add the cranberries which have been washed. Beat the egg and add to the milk, then add this slowly to the dry ingredients. Add the melted butter and mix well. Pour into 8 individual molds which have been buttered, and place in the oven in a steamer with about 1½ inches of boiling water in it. Be sure the steamer is covered, but do not cover the molds. Let steam at 400 degrees for 1 hour.

Yield: 8 servings.

DATE PUDDING

Temperature, 400 degrees; Time, 1 hour

or

Temperature, 275 degrees; Time, 3 hours*

¼ cup butter	3 cups stale bread crumbs
¾ cup sugar	1 pound dates
1 egg	4 tablespoons flour
½ cup milk	2 teaspoons baking powder

Cream the butter and sugar. Stir in the egg which has been beaten and mixed with the milk. Add the stale bread crumbs and the dates which have been washed, pitted and cut into small pieces. Then sift in the flour with the baking powder. Beat well to mix thoroughly. A teaspoon of cinnamon may be added if desired. Pour the batter into 2 well-greased molds 3½ x 4½ inches and steam in the oven by placing the mold in a pan or roaster containing about 1½ inches of boiling water. Cover the pan but not the molds. Use either of the temperatures for the length of time given above. Serve with Hard Sauce (see page 114).

Yield: 6 servings.

DATE AND WALNUT TORTE

Temperature, 325 degrees; Time, 40 to 45 minutes

2 eggs	⅛ teaspoon salt
½ cup brown sugar	½ cup walnut meats
2 tablespoons flour	½ cup dates
1 teaspoon baking powder	¼ teaspoon vanilla

Beat the eggs very light and add the sugar. Continue beating and then add the flour sifted with the baking powder and salt. Lastly add the broken nut meats and dates, which have been stoned and cut into pieces. Add the vanilla. Bake at 325 degrees for 40 to 45 minutes. Serve with sweetened whipped cream.

Yield: 5 servings.

---

* This time and temperature is suitable for oven meals.

HUCKLEBERRY PUDDING

Temperature, 400 degrees; Time, 1 hour

or

Temperature, 275 degrees; Time, 3 hours*

1½ cups flour
2 teaspoons baking powder
½ teaspoon salt
¼ cup sugar

2 cups huckleberries
½ cup milk
3 tablespoons butter

Sift the dry ingredients together and add the huckleberries which have been washed and stemmed. Then stir in the milk and butter which has been melted. Turn into 2 well-greased molds 3½ x 4½ inches. Place in a pan containing 1½ inches of boiling water. Cover the pan but not the molds. Steam in the oven at either of the above temperatures.

Yield: 6 servings.

INDIAN PUDDING

Temperature, 400 degrees; Time, 30 minutes

or

Temperature, 275 degrees; Time, 3 hours*

1 pint milk
3 tablespoons cornmeal
2 tablespoons butter
3 tablespoons molasses
¼ teaspoon ginger

¼ teaspoon nutmeg
¼ teaspoon cinnamon
½ teaspoon salt
¼ cup sugar
2 eggs

Heat the milk in the top of a double boiler. Then add the cornmeal and cook over boiling water for 15 minutes. Add the remaining ingredients together with the well-beaten eggs. Mix well and pour into a buttered baking dish. Bake at either of the above temperatures. If it is desirable to use the whole meal temperature cover the pudding and place it in a shallow pan containing about 1½ inches of boiling water.

Yield: 6 servings.

---

* This time and temperature is suitable for oven meals.

FRENCH PASTRIES WEAR A PROFESSIONAL LOOK

LEMON PIE IS THE ACME OF DELICIOUSNESS

PLUM PUDDING

Temperature, 275 degrees; Time, 3 hours

⅓ cup butter
1 cup brown sugar
4 eggs
1 teaspoon salt
2 teaspoons baking powder
½ teaspoon cinnamon

4 tablespoons flour
½ pound raisins
2 ounces citron
½ cup walnut meats
1 orange rind, grated
2½ cups bread crumbs

Cream the butter and add the sugar, then the well-beaten eggs. Sift the salt, baking powder, cinnamon and flour together. Add the chopped raisins, citron, finely broken walnut meats, orange rind and soft bread crumbs to the dry ingredients. Combine these mixtures, being sure they are well blended. Pour into well-buttered individual molds 2½ x 2¾ inches, or 1 large mold 3¾ x 5¾ inches. Place on a rack in a pan containing about 1½ inches of boiling water. Cover the large mold but not the small ones and also cover the pan containing the boiling water. Bake at 275 degrees for 3 hours.

These puddings will keep and can be made in advance and then reheated for the meal at which they are to be served.

Yield: 8 servings.

RASPBERRY PUDDING

Temperature, 275 degrees; Time, 3 hours

¼ cup butter
½ cup sugar
3 eggs
2 tablespoons flour

3 cups bread crumbs
¼ teaspoon salt
3 tablespoons raspberry
  jam

Cream the butter and sugar and add the well-beaten eggs. Then add the flour, bread crumbs, salt and jam. Mix well and pour into a buttered mold. Place in a large pan containing boiling water to a depth of 1½ inches. Cover the pan but not the mold. Steam in the oven at 275 degrees for 3 hours.

Yield: 6 servings.

CREAMY RICE PUDDING

Temperature, 300 degrees; Time, 2¼ hours

⅓ cup uncooked rice	3½ cups milk
¼ teaspoon salt	¼ teaspoon cinnamon
¼ cup sugar	½ teaspoon vanilla

Wash the rice thoroughly and mix all the ingredients together in a buttered baking pan. Place in the oven at 300 degrees for 2¼ hours.

Yield: 6 servings.

RICE PUDDING

Temperature, 350 degrees; Time, 1 hour

2 eggs	1 teaspoon vanilla
⅓ cup sugar	2½ cups boiled rice
¼ teaspoon salt	2 cups milk

Beat the eggs slightly and add the sugar, salt and vanilla. Then add the rice and milk. Pour into a buttered dish and place it in a shallow pan with about 1½ inches of boiling water in it. Bake at 350 degrees for about 1 hour.

Yield: 6 servings.

TAPIOCA CREAM

Temperature, 300 degrees; Time, 20 minutes

1 pint milk	¼ cup sugar
4 tablespoons granulated tapioca	⅛ teaspoon salt
2 egg yolks	½ teaspoon vanilla

Scald the milk over hot water. Add the tapioca and cook for 15 minutes, stirring constantly. Beat the egg yolks and add the sugar and salt to them. Add a little of the hot tapioca and milk to the egg mixture and pour this into the rest of the tapioca mixture. Stir and cook until thick. Add the vanilla and remove from the fire. Pour into a buttered baking dish and spread the following meringue over the top of it:

Meringue

2 egg whites   ½ teaspoon vanilla
4 tablespoons sugar

Beat the egg whites and add the sugar gradually, then the vanilla. Spread over the Tapioca Cream and put it in the oven at 300 degrees for 20 minutes.

If desired, the pudding dish may be lined with stale sponge cake before putting the tapioca in it. This dessert may be served with currant jelly or cream, either plain or whipped.

Yield: 6 servings.

❈   ●   ●   ❈

Soufflés

VANILLA SOUFFLÉ

Temperature, 325 degrees; Time, 1 hour

4 tablespoons butter   ⅓ cup sugar
5 tablespoons flour   1 teaspoon vanilla
¼ teaspoon salt   3 eggs
1 cup milk

Make a sauce by heating the butter and adding the flour slowly. Stir constantly. Then add the salt and milk, stirring while adding. Cook until smooth and thickened. Cool and add the sugar, vanilla and egg yolks which have been beaten to a yellow cream color. Then carefully fold in the stiffly beaten egg whites. Pour this mixture into a well-buttered baking dish. Place the baking dish, uncovered, in a pan which contains about 1 inch of boiling water. Bake at 325 degrees for 1 hour.

One cup of almonds, blanched and broken; 1 cup of dates, stoned and cut, or 1 cup of shredded cocoanut, may be added to the recipe for Vanilla Soufflé for variation. They should be mixed into the other ingredients before the egg whites are folded in.

For Chocolate Soufflé use 2 ounces of melted chocolate. Add the sugar and salt. Cool, then add to the sauce made as directed above.

Yield: 6 servings.

ORANGE SOUFFLÉ

Temperature, 325 degrees; Time, 1 hour

1 cup milk	⅓ cup sugar
5 tablespoons flour	½ orange rind, grated
4 tablespoons butter	3 tablespoons orange juice
3 egg yolks	1 tablespoon lemon juice
¼ teaspoon salt	3 egg whites

Make a sauce of the butter, flour and milk according to the directions given in Vanilla Souffle (see page 63). Cool and add the beaten egg yolks, salt and sugar. Add the orange and lemon juice and rind. Then fold in the beaten egg whites. Bake in a buttered baking dish placed in a pan containing 1 inch of boiling water at 325 degrees for 1 hour.

Yield: 6 servings.

RICE SOUFFLÉ

Temperature, 325 degrees; Time, 1 hour

⅓ cup rice	4 tablespoons butter
1½ cups milk	⅓ cup sugar
½ lemon rind, grated	¼ teaspoon salt
1 cup milk	3 eggs
5 tablespoons flour	

Cook the rice with the 1½ cups of milk over hot water until it is tender. Add it and the lemon rind to the sauce using the above proportions and made according to the directions given for Vanilla Souffle (see page 63). Add the sugar and salt. Fold in the egg whites. Turn into a buttered baking dish and place the dish in a pan containing about 1 inch of boiling water. Bake uncovered at 325 degrees for 1 hour.

Yield: 6 servings.

CHAPTER VI

FISH

From the very wide variety of fish available at all seasons of the year and in practically every locality it should appear more often on the menus in every home. Some varieties are especially fine for broiling but practically every variety may be baked.

The Spencer method is one of the best methods to use for preparing fish, although if the fish is large enough, or the piece is thick enough, it may be prepared whole meal style. For the Spencer method the fish should be dipped into a bowl of salted milk, then in fine bread crumbs or cracker crumbs, and placed on a well-oiled pan with some oil put over the top. It should then be put into a hot oven and baked for a comparatively short time.

For the whole meal style it may be put into a slow oven with the rest of the meal.

BAKED STUFFED FISH

Temperature, 400 degrees; Time, 1 hour
or
Temperature, 500 degrees for searing; Time, 20 minutes
then
Temperature, 275 degrees; Time, 3 hours*

1 3–pound white fish	3 cups stale bread cubes
1 onion, chopped	1½ teaspoons salt
1 tablespoon parsley, chopped	⅛ teaspoon pepper
	1 egg
2 tablespoons butter	½ cup boiling water

Brown the onion and parsley in the butter and mix with the crumbs, seasonings, and egg. Wipe the fish and sprinkle the inside with salt and pepper. Put the stuffing in it. Hold it together with skewers or sew it. Place on a greased rack in a roaster and sear at 500 degrees for 20 minutes. Add the boiling water and cover. Leave the valve in the cover open. Bake at 275 degrees for 3 hours, or at 400 degrees for 1 hour without searing.

Yield: 5 servings.

---

* This time and temperature is suitable for oven meals.

DEVILLED CRAB MEAT

Temperature, 400 degrees; Time, 15 to 18 minutes

2 tablespoons butter
2½ tablespoons flour
1 cup milk
2 cups canned crab meat
1 teaspoon salt

¼ teaspoon paprika
⅟₁₆ teaspoon cayenne
2 tablespoons lemon
   juice
1 cup buttered crumbs

Melt the butter and add the flour. Then stir in the heated milk slowly to make a white sauce. Add the crab meat mixed with the seasonings. Put into greased individual ramekins. Put the buttered crumbs on top and bake at 400 degrees for 15 to 18 minutes. Two hard cooked eggs may be chopped and added to the crab meat. One tablespoon of Worcestershire Sauce may be added to the sauce.

Yield: 5 servings.

BAKED FILLET OF HADDOCK

(Fresh or Smoked)

Temperature, 450 degrees; Time, 25 minutes

1 3–pound haddock, fillet
½ teaspoon salt

½ cup milk
⅓ cup cracker crumbs
1 teaspoon oil

Mix the salt and milk and dip the fish into this. Then roll it in the cracker crumbs. See that it is well covered with the crumbs. Place it in a well-oiled baking pan and put 1 teaspoon of oil over the top. Bake at 450 degrees for 25 minutes.

Yield: 5 servings.

HALIBUT STEAK

Temperature, 450 degrees; Time, 35 minutes

or

Temperature, 500 degrees for searing; Time, 20 minutes

then

Temperature, 275 degrees; Time, 3 hours*

2 tablespoons oil
1 onion

2 pounds halibut steak, 2½
  inches thick
2 ounces salt pork

Put 2 tablespoons of oil in a shallow pan Slice the onion and place the halibut steak on it in the pan. Put the sliced salt pork over the top or use another tablespoon of oil in its place. If oil is used add 1 teaspoon of salt. Bake at 450 degrees for 35 minutes. If it is desired to use the whole meal temperature sear at 500 degrees for 20 minutes, then cover and bake at 275 degrees for 3 hours.

Yield: 5 servings.

SCALLOPED HALIBUT

Temperature, 400 degrees; Time, 30 minutes

2 cups milk
4 tablespoons flour
3 tablespoons butter
1½ teaspoons salt
⅛ teaspoon paprika

3 cups halibut (cooked)
1½ cups potatoes (cooked)
2 hard cooked eggs
2 cups bread crumbs
2 tablespoons butter

Make a white sauce of the milk, flour, butter, salt and paprika as given under Devilled Crab Meat on p. 66. Into a well-buttered baking dish put half of the flaked halibut and diced potatoes. Slice the hard-cooked eggs and put over this, then add about half of the white sauce. Repeat with the rest of the ingredients, putting the buttered soft bread crumbs on last. Bake at 400 degrees for 30 minutes.

Yield: 6 Servings.

---

* This time and temperature is suitable for oven meals.

OYSTERS AND MUSHROOMS IN TOAST BOXES

Temperature, 450 degrees; Time, 15 to 20 minutes

Cut a loaf of bread into cubes about 3½ inches square. Remove the centers of the cubes, and butter. Remove the stems and wash the large mushrooms. Brown them in butter, and put one or two of them in the bottom of the opening in each toast box. Put two large oysters on top and sprinkle with salt and pepper. Place in a baking dish and bake at 450 degrees for 15 to 20 minutes.

BAKED SALMON

Temperature, 450 degrees; Time, 30 to 35 minutes

½ teaspoon salt	⅔ cup cracker crumbs
½ cup milk	2 pounds of salmon steaks

Put the salt into the milk and dip the steaks into this, then into the cracker crumbs. Place in a well-oiled baking dish and put a small amount of oil on top of each steak. Bake at 450 degrees for 30 to 35 minutes.

Yield: 5 servings.

BAKED SHAD

Temperature, 450 degrees; Time, 35 to 40 minutes

1 shad	⅛ teaspoon pepper
½ teaspoon salt	1 tablespoon butter

Place the cleaned shad in a well-oiled baking dish. Sprinkle with the salt and pepper. Brush over with the melted butter and bake at 450 degrees for 35 to 40 minutes.

Yield: 5 servings.

BAKED SHAD ROE

Temperature, 450 degrees; Time, 15 minutes

1 roe
¼ cup milk
¼ teaspoon salt

⅓ cup cracker crumbs
⅓ cup butter

Add the salt to the milk and dip the roe into it. Then dip
it into the finely ground cracker crumbs. Place in a well-buttered
baking dish and sprinkle liberally with melted butter. Bake at
450 degrees for 15 minutes. Serve with Maître d'Hôtel Dressing
(see p. 117). Put in the oven 15 minutes before the shad has
finished baking.

BAKED SHRIMP

Temperature, 450 degrees; Time, 20 minutes

1½ pints shrimp (boiled or
  canned)
1 cup cream

½ teaspoon salt
¼ teaspoon paprika
1½ tablespoons butter

Put the shrimps in boiling water for about 3 minutes. Drain
and put into a greased baking dish. Add the remaining ingredients and bake at 450 degrees for 20 minutes.

Yield: 6 servings.

CHAPTER VII

MEATS AND MEAT SUBSTITUTES

Meats

There is a great variation in the quality of meat. Methods of animal feeding and amount of fat, bone and connective tissue in the meat contribute to its quality. These factors will influence the length of time necessary to cook meat to the desired condition.

Because people differ in their standards of rare, medium rare, and well done, it may be desirable to change some of the lengths of time for roasting.

Meat should be seared at a high temperature (450 to 500 degrees) to prevent loss of the juices. This process may be accomplished in the oven, in the broiler, or over a surface burner. Continue the cooking at a reduced temperature (275 degrees) so that the heat will penetrate evenly to the center of the roast.

Roasts may be placed on a rack in a roasting pan without adding water and without covering. The fat will baste the meat as the heat melts it and it runs over the surface to the bottom of the pan.

Some people prefer to cover the meat while it is being baked. The steam from the cooking helps it cook in a shorter time than when cooked entirely by dry heat, although it changes the flavor somewhat.

BACON

Temperature, 400 degrees; Time, 15 to 17 minutes

Allow three or four slices of bacon for each person. Put the strips of bacon on a rack in a shallow baking pan. Put it in the oven at 400 degrees for 15 to 17 minutes.

BRAISED BEEF (Tough Cuts)

(Chuck-rib or Shoulder, Rump, English Cut, Round)

Temperature, 500 degrees for searing; Time, 20 to 30 minutes
then
Temperature, 275 degrees; Time, 3 hours

4 or 5 pounds beef   1 tablespoon salt
1 cup boiling water

Put the meat on a rack in a roasting pan and place it, uncovered, in the oven to sear at 500 degrees for 20 to 30 minutes. Remove it from the oven and pour 1 cup of boiling water in the bottom of the pan. Sprinkle the salt over the meat. Cover and bake at 275 degrees for 3 hours.

BEEF LOAF

Temperature, 400 degrees; Time, 45 minutes
or
Temperature, 275 degrees; Time, 3 hours*

1½ pounds ground beef   ¾ cup milk
1 cup cracker crumbs   1 egg
1½ tablespoons chopped   2 tablespoons Worcester-
    onion   shire Sauce
2 teaspoons salt   1 tablespoon butter
½ teaspoon pepper

Mix all the ingredients together except the butter. Place in a loaf pan, 4½ x 8 inches, cover with the tablespoon of butter and bake at either of the above temperatures.

---

* This time and temperature is suitable for oven meals.

ROAST BEEF

Temperature, 500 degrees for searing; Time, 20 to 30 minutes
then
Temperature, 275 degrees; Time, 3 hours

8 pounds rib roast, unboned   ½ teaspoon pepper
2 tablespoons salt

Place the meat on a rack in a roaster and sear at 500 degrees for 20 to 30 minutes. Then sprinkle it with the salt and pepper. Bake uncovered at 275 degrees for 3 hours.

For a smaller roast sear at 500 degrees for 20 to 30 minutes and then bake it at 275 degrees for 15 minutes per pound if desired rare; 18 minutes per pound for medium rare; and 20 to 22 minutes per pound for well done.

BEEF STEW

Temperature, 500 degrees for searing; Time, 20 minutes
then
Temperature, 275 degrees; Time, 3 hours

2 pounds beef, round or rump   1 bunch celery
6 potatoes   1 tablespoon salt
6 white turnips   ¼ teaspoon pepper
3 onions   2½ cups boiling water
6 carrots

Cut the beef into cubes and sear it in a casserole at 500 degrees for 20 minutes while preparing the vegetables. Cut the medium size vegetables into dice and slice the onions. Put them in the casserole with the meat, seasonings, and boiling water, at the end of the 20 minutes. Cover and bake at 275 degrees for 3 hours.

BAKED HAM

Temperature, 500 degrees for searing; Time, 20 to 30 minutes
then
Temperature, 275 degrees; Time, 4 hours

1 12–pound high grade ham

Wash the ham well. Wipe dry and place in a roaster. Sear at 500 degrees for 20 to 30 minutes. Cover and bake at 275 degrees for 4 hours.

BAKED HAM WITH CIDER

Temperature, 500 degrees for searing; Time, 20 to 30 minutes
then
Temperature, 275 degrees; Time, 3 hours

1 12–pound high grade ham   1 cup brown sugar
2 onions   2 quarts cider
20 cloves

Wash the ham well with a brush and cut a slit in both ends. Insert a small onion in the slit in each end and put the ham in a roaster. Sear at 500 degrees for 20 to 30 minutes. Then insert the cloves over the top, and cover with the brown sugar. Other seasonings such as bay leaf or thyme may be used if desired. Pour the cider around it and cover. Bake at 275 degrees for 3 hours.

BAKED FRESH HAM

Temperature, 500 degrees for searing; Time, 20 to 30 minutes
then
Temperature, 350 degrees; Time, 30 minutes per pound

Place the ham on a rack in a roaster and sear at 500 degrees for 20 to 30 minutes. Then sprinkle with salt and pepper and continue baking, uncovered, at 350 degrees for 30 minutes per pound.

BOILED HAM

Temperature, 275 degrees; Time, 20 minutes per pound

Wash the ham well. Place in a kettle or roasting pan. Cover the ham with water, or fill the pan at least three quarters full. Place over a surface burner. Cover and heat until it reaches the boiling point. Then immediately place it in the oven at 275 degrees for 20 minutes per pound.

If the ham is cooked in a roasting pan turn the meat when the cooking period is about half over. When the cooking period is completed remove the ham from the oven and unless it is to be served hot let it remain in the water in which it was cooked until it is cold.

BONED SMOKED SHOULDER OF PORK

*Temperature, 500 degrees for searing; Time, 15 to 20 minutes
then*

Temperature, 275 degrees; Time, 3 hours

3½ to 4-pound boned shoulder   10 whole cloves
¼ cup brown sugar   ½ cup boiling water

Wash the meat and rub it with brown sugar. Insert the cloves, distributing them equally. Put the ham on a rack in a roasting pan and place in the oven at 500 degrees for 15 to 20 minutes to brown. Then add ½ cup of boiling water, cover the roaster and bake at 275 degrees for 3 hours.

BOILED BONED SMOKED SHOULDER OF PORK

Temperature, 275 degrees; Time, 3 hours

Wash the meat and put it in a pan. Stick with cloves. Cover with boiling water. Put an onion or clove of garlic in the water. Cover and bake at 275 degrees for 3 hours.

BAKED CALVES' HEARTS

Temperature, 400 degrees; Time, 1½ hours
or
Temperature, 275 degrees; Time, 3 hours*

2 calves' hearts
1 cup bread crumbs
¼ teaspoon salt

1 tablespoon onion
1 tablespoon butter
1 cup boiling water

Wash the hearts well and remove the large veins and connective tissue. Stuff them with a mixture of soft bread crumbs, salt, chopped onion, and melted butter. Place on a rack in a baking dish. Add the water and bake at either of the above temperatures.

BAKED LAMB CHOPS

Temperature, 400 degrees; Time, 50 minutes

6 or more chops
½ teaspoon salt

⅛ teaspoon pepper

Select lamb chops about 1½ inches thick and place them in a baking dish. Sprinkle with the salt and pepper. Bake at 400 degrees for 50 minutes.

ROAST LEG OF LAMB

Temperature, 350 degrees; Time, 30 minutes per pound
or
Temperature, 500 degrees for searing; Time, 20 to 30 minutes
then
Temperature, 275 degrees; Time, 3 hours*

5-pound leg of lamb
2 teaspoons salt

¼ teaspoon pepper
1½ cups boiling water

Put the meat on a rack in a roaster. Sear at 500 degrees for 20 to 30 minutes. Season and bake at 275 degrees for 3 hours, or at 350 degrees for 30 minutes per pound. If covered, let the valve in the cover of the roaster open. At the end of the baking time remove the meat from the pan and pour the boiling water into the pan. Thicken the gravy with 1½ tablespoons of flour mixed with a little cold water for each cup of liquid. Cook over a surface burner, stirring constantly.

---

* This time and temperature is suitable for oven meals.

LAMB STEW

Temperature, 275 degrees; Time, 3 hours

2 pounds stewing lamb	1 cup carrots
1 onion	1 green pepper, chopped
3 tablespoons fat	1 tablespoon salt
2 cups potatoes	1/8 teaspoon pepper
2 cups turnips	1 cup boiling water

Shoulder of lamb will make a good stew. Have it cut in 1½-inch cubes. Sear with the chopped onion in the heated fat over a surface burner. Then add the vegetables, which have been cubed, and the seasonings. Pour the boiling water over it, and bake at 275 degrees for 3 hours.

BAKED LIVER

Temperature, 400 degrees; Time, 25 to 30 minutes

Have calf's liver cut at least ¼ inch thick. Place slices side by side on a well-buttered shallow baking dish. Put bits of butter over the top and bake at 400 degrees for 25 to 30 minutes.

CASSEROLE OF LIVER

Temperature, 500 degrees for searing; Time, 20 minutes
then
Temperature, 275 degrees; Time, 3 hours

1½ pounds liver	½ green pepper
2 onions	½ red pepper
2 slices bacon	1½ cups strained tomato
¾ cup spaghetti	2 teaspoons salt

Place the piece of liver and the onions, which have been sliced, in a casserole. Lay slices of bacon over the liver. Place in the oven at 500 degrees for 20 minutes. Cook the spaghetti in boiling water for about 8 minutes over a surface burner. Drain and add to the liver. Then add the peppers, which have been sliced; the tomato and salt. Cover and cook at 275 degrees for 3 hours.

BAKED HAM MAKES A REAL MEAL EITHER FOR
COMPANY OR JUST "FAMILY FOLKS"

A Brown and Juicy Turkey Necessitates Lots of
Accompaniments

BREADED PORK CHOPS

Temperature, 400 degrees; Time, 50 minutes

or

Temperature, 275 degrees; Time, 3 hours*

6 or more pork chops	1 egg
¾ cup fine crumbs	¼ cup milk
1 teaspoon salt	¼ cup boiling water
⅛ teaspoon pepper	

Add the salt and pepper to the fine bread or cracker crumbs. Beat the egg and add the milk. Dip the chops into this, then into the crumbs. Brown in a frying pan on a surface burner. Put in a baking dish and add ¼ cup of boiling water. Cover and bake at either of the above temperatures.

ROAST PORK LOIN

Temperature, 500 degrees for searing; Time, 20 to 30 minutes

then

Temperature, 275 degrees; Time, 3 hours

4 or 5–pound pork loin	⅛ teaspoon pepper
2 teaspoons salt	

Place the roast on a rack in a roasting pan. Sear at 500 degrees for 20 to 30 minutes. Sprinkle with salt and pepper. Bake either covered or uncovered at 275 degrees for 3 hours. The same directions for baking will apply to a boned shoulder of pork.

---

* This time and temperature is suitable for oven meals.

POT ROAST

Temperature, 500 degrees for searing; Time, 20 to 30 minutes
then
Temperature, 350 degrees; Time, 2 hours
or
*Temperature, 275 degrees; Time, 3 hours**

3½ pounds beef rump   ⅛ teaspoon pepper
1 onion   ½ cup boiling water
1½ teaspoons salt

Place the meat and the sliced onion in a baking dish and sear at 500 degrees for 20 to 30 minutes. Add the salt, pepper and boiling water. Cover and bake at 350 degrees for 2 hours, or at 275 degrees for 3 hours.

BAKED SAUSAGE

Temperature, 400 degrees; Time, 25 to 30 minutes

1 or more pounds sausage

Place the sausage, either links or cakes, on a rack in a roaster or pan. Do not let the pieces overlap. Prick each link with a fork. Bake at 400 degrees for 25 to 30 minutes.

SAUSAGE LOAF

Temperature, 400 degrees; Time, 1 hour

2 cups sausage meat   1 teaspoon salt
1 cup stewed tomatoes   ¼ teaspoon pepper
2 cups mashed potatoes   1 egg
2 cups bread crumbs

Combine all of the ingredients thoroughly, adding the well-beaten egg last. Place in a loaf pan and bake at 400 degrees for 1 hour. If it is not brown enough at the end of that time allow 5 minutes more.

* This time and temperature is suitable for oven meals.

BAKED PORTERHOUSE STEAK

Temperature, 500 degrees for searing; Time, 20 minutes
then
Temperature, 275 degrees; Time, 30 to 35 minutes

3½ pounds porterhouse steak   1 teaspoon salt
    2½ inches thick   ⅛ teaspoon pepper

Trim the meat and place the steak on a rack in a roaster. Sear at 500 degrees for 20 minutes. Then sprinkle with salt and pepper and bake at 275 degrees for 30 to 35 minutes.

TOMATO STEAK

Temperature, 500 degrees for searing; Time, 20 minutes
then
Temperature, 275 degrees; Time, 3 hours

3 pounds round steak   2 cloves
    2 inches thick   2 teaspoons salt
1 pint tomatoes   ⅛ teaspoon pepper
2 carrots   2 tablespoons flour
1 large onion   2 tablespoons water
1 turnip

Score the beef by slashing with a sharp knife. Place it in a casserole and sear at 500 degrees for 20 minutes. Prepare the vegetables and put them through the coarse knife of the food chopper. Add them and the seasonings to the meat. Cover and bake at 275 degrees for 3 hours. Remove from the oven. Add the 2 tablespoons of flour mixed with 2 tablespoons of water. Boil together over a surface burner for a few minutes until thickened enough for gravy,

VEAL BIRDS

Temperature, 400 degrees; Time, 1 hour
or
Temperature, 275 degrees; Time, 3 hours*

1½ pounds veal steak sliced thin	2 tablespoons butter
	2 tablespoons flour
¼ cup flour	1½ cups boiling water

Wash the veal and trim off the fat. Cut it into 6 pieces of uniform size and rectangular in shape. Spread each piece with stuffing.

Stuffing

2 ounces salt pork	⅛ teaspoon thyme
1 egg	½ onion, scraped
1 teaspoon salt	2 tablespoons lemon
¾ teaspoon celery salt	juice
⅛ teaspoon pepper	¾ cup bread crumbs

Put the salt pork through the food chopper. Add the well-beaten egg. Mix in the other ingredients. Divide into as many portions as there are pieces of veal. Roll into little rolls, holding in shape with skewers. Roll the "birds" in the ¼ cup flour and brown in the 2 tablespoons of melted butter over a surface burner. Add 2 tablespoons of flour to the fat in the pan, stirring to prevent lumps. Add 1½ cups of boiling water and put in a casserole. Cover and bake at either of the above temperatures.

VEAL CUTLETS

Temperature, 500 degrees for searing; Time, 15 minutes
then
Temperature, 400 degrees; Time, 50 minutes
or
Temperature, 275 degrees; Time, 3 hours*

1½ pounds veal steak	1 teaspoon salt
1 egg	1 cup cracker crumbs
⅓ cup milk	1 cup boiling water

* This time and temperature is suitable for oven meals.

Beat the egg slightly. Add the milk and salt. Cut the veal into pieces for serving and dip each piece into the egg and milk mixture. Then dip it into the cracker crumbs. Place in a greased casserole and put in the oven at 500 degrees for 15 minutes to sear. Add 1 cup of boiling water, cover, and bake at either of the above temperatures.

VEAL LOAF

Temperature, 400 degrees; Time, 40 to 50 minutes

1½ pounds ground veal
¼ cup cracker crumbs
1 tablespoon lemon juice
1½ teaspoons salt
½ teaspoon pepper
4 tablespoons milk
⅛ teaspoon onion juice

Mix all the ingredients and place in a greased loaf pan. Spread with 1 tablespoon of butter and place in the oven at 400 degrees for 40 to 50 minutes.

ROAST VEAL

Temperature, 500 degrees for searing; Time, 20 to 30 minutes
then
Temperature, 275 degrees; Time, 3 hours

5–pound rump roast of veal
2 cups bread cubes
2 tablespoons butter
½ onion
½ teaspoon salt
⅛ teaspoon pepper
¼ teaspoon marjoram
½ teaspoon chopped parsley
1 tablespoon chopped green pepper

Have a pocket cut in the roast. Fill it with a filling made by mixing the stale bread cubes, melted butter, chopped onion, and seasonings together. Place on a rack in a roaster. Sear at 500 degrees for 20 to 30 minutes. Sprinkle with salt and pepper, cover, and bake at 275 degrees for 3 hours.

Meat Substitutes and Extenders

BEEF BALLS EN CASSEROLE

Temperature, 350 degrees; Time, 1 hour

or

Temperature, 275 degrees; Time, 3 hours*

1 pound round steak, ground	½ teaspoon salt
¼ cup bread crumbs	¼ teaspoon paprika
1 egg	

Mix all of the ingredients thoroughly. Then divide into 6 portions and roll each into a compact ball. Sear in a small amount of fat in a frying pan. Place in a casserole with the following vegetables:

6 potatoes	½ green pepper, sliced
6 onions	1½ teaspoons salt
½ can or 1 cup tomatoes	

Cover and bake at either of the above temperatures.

Yield: 6 servings.

CHEESE SOUFFLÉ

Temperature, 325 degrees; Time, 1 hour

4 tablespoons butter	½ teaspoon salt
5 tablespoons flour	½ cup cheese
1 cup milk	3 eggs

Melt the butter and stir in the flour. Gradually add the milk, stirring constantly. Add the salt and cheese which has been grated or cut in small cubes. Cook and stir until the cheese is melted. Cool and add the beaten egg yolks, then fold in the stiffly-beaten egg whites. Pour into a well-greased baking dish set in a pan containing 1 inch of boiling water and bake at 325 degrees for 1 hour.

* This time and temperature is suitable for oven meals.

This recipe may be varied by using 1 cup of strained tomato instead of the milk. One cup of previously cooked corn or other vegetable may be used instead of the ½ cup of cheese. Fresh corn is usually drier than canned, so if the canned corn is used let it drain in order that it contain as little liquid as possible. Too much liquid in a soufflé will have a tendency to make it soggy rather than light and fluffy.

Yield: 6 servings.

CHICKEN CURRY

Temperature, 375 degrees; Time, 1¼ hours

2 cups chicken	1 teaspoon salt
1½ cups celery	1 teaspoon curry powder
¾ cup rice	3½ cups liquid

Cube pieces of previously cooked chicken and put in a casserole with pieces of celery, uncooked rice and the seasonings. Add the boiling liquid, which may be either milk or gravy and water. Cover and bake at 375 degrees for 1¼ hours.

Yield: 6 servings.

CHICKEN LOAF

Temperature, 400 degrees; Time, 45 minutes

3 cups chicken	2 egg yolks
1 cup carrots	2 teaspoons salt
1½ cups peas	2 teaspoons onion juice
1½ cups bread crumbs	1 teaspoon lemon juice
1 cup milk	

This loaf is made of previously cooked chicken and vegetables. Leftovers may be used. Put the chicken, carrots, and peas through the grinder, using a coarse knife. Add the rest of the ingredients. Mix together and place in a greased loaf pan. Bake at 400 degrees for 45 minutes.

Yield: 6 servings.

CHICKEN TIMBALES

Temperature, 400 degrees; Time, ½ hour

4 eggs
1 teaspoon onion juice
1 teaspoon salt
⅛ teaspoon pepper

1 tablespoon parsley
1 cup milk
2¼ cups previously
    cooked chicken

Beat the eggs and add the onion juice, seasonings and milk. Then add the diced chicken. Pour into individual custard cups and place them in a shallow pan of boiling water. Bake at 400 degrees for ½ hour. These timbales are especially desirable when served with a mushroom sauce.

Yield: 6 servings.

CHICKEN AND CORN CASSEROLE

Temperature, 400 degrees; Time, 40 minutes

2½ cups chicken
3½ cups corn
2 tablespoons butter
½ onion
2 tablespoons flour

1½ cups milk
1½ teaspoons salt
⅛ teaspoon pepper
⅛ teaspoon paprika

Arrange cubes of previously cooked chicken and the corn cut from the cob in a casserole in alternating layers. Melt the butter and to it add the chopped onion. Cook slightly, then add the flour mixed with the milk. Stir until thick and add the seasonings. Pour over the corn and chicken and bake at 400 degrees for 40 minutes.

Yield: 6 servings.

CHILI CON CARNE

Temperature, 300 degrees; Time, 3½ hours

1 pint dry kidney beans	1 tablespoon salt
1 pound ground beef	1 tablespoon chili powder
1 onion	¼ teaspoon thyme
2 tablespoons fat	⅛ teaspoon cloves
1 pint tomatoes	1½ pints water or
2 teaspoons flour	meat or vegetable
½ cup uncooked rice	stock

Soak the kidney beans over night. Then brown the chopped meat and onion in the fat in a sauce pan over a surface burner. Mix the canned tomatoes and flour together and add them to the meat. Then add the remaining ingredients and cook until it reaches the boiling point. Cover and place in the oven at 300 degrees for 3½ hours.

Yield: 6 servings.

CHOP SUEY (American)

Temperature, 350 degrees; Time, 1½ hours
or
Temperature, 275 degrees; Time, 2½ hours

1 pound fresh lean pork	1½ cups mushrooms
4 onions	1¾ teaspoons salt
½ tablespoon fat	½ cup rice
3 cups celery	3 cups meat or vegetable
2 green peppers	stock

Cut the pork into small pieces and slice the onions very thin. Brown in a pan with the fat. Place in a baking dish and add the celery, peppers and mushrooms. Then add the rest of the ingredients. Part of the stock may be made by boiling the stems and skins of the mushrooms in 2 cups of water for 10 or 15 minutes. Bake in a covered pan at 350 degrees for 1½ hours or at 275 degrees for 2½ hours.

Yield: 6 servings.

BAKED LAMB CROQUETTES

Temperature, 425 degrees; Time, 45 minutes

2 tablespoons butter	2½ cups lamb (left over)
4 tablespoons flour	1 tablespoon parsley
½ teaspoon salt	⅛ teaspoon paprika
1 cup milk	½ teaspoon lemon juice

Melt the butter and stir in the flour and salt. Add the milk gradually. Continue stirring until smooth. Chop the lamb and parsley, and with the paprika and lemon juice, add to the sauce. Let cool and shape in flat balls. Roll in cracker crumbs, then in the egg, then again in the cracker crumbs until the croquettes are well coated. Place on a well buttered shallow baking dish. Bake at 425 degrees for 45 minutes, turning after they have been in the oven for 20 minutes.

Yield: 6 servings.

MACARONI AND CHEESE

Temperature, 350 degrees; Time, 50 minutes

1½ cups elbow macaroni	1 teaspoon salt
¼ cup butter	⅛ teaspoon pepper
1½ cups American cheese	½ teaspoon paprika
1½ tablespoons onion	2 eggs
1½ tablespoons parsley	2 cups milk
1½ tablespoons pimiento	

Cook the macaroni in boiling salted water for 15 minutes. Drain and pour cold water through it. Put it in a buttered baking dish. Add the butter, cubed cheese, chopped onion, parsley, pimiento and seasonings to the macaroni. Beat the eggs slightly and add the hot milk to them. Pour over the macaroni and cheese and bake, uncovered, at 350 degrees for 50 minutes. This may be served with Mushroom Sauce (see p. 117).

Yield: 6 servings.

MEAT PIE

Temperature, 275 degrees; Time, 2½ hours
then
Temperature, 400 degrees; Time, ½ hour

1½ pounds stewing lamb	1 cup carrots
3 tablespoons onion	1 cup water
3 tablespoons fat	1 tablespoon salt
2 cups potatoes	⅛ teaspoon pepper
2 cups turnips	

For Crust

1½ cups flour	3 tablespoons fat
3 teaspoons baking powder	⅝ cup milk
1 teaspoon salt	

Have the meat cut into inch cubes. Wash well and sear it with the chopped onion in the fat. Put it with the cubed vegetables, water and seasonings in a baking dish. Place in the oven at 275 degrees for 2½ hours. For the crust sift the flour, baking powder and salt together. Cut in the fat. Add the milk and mix lightly. At the end of the 2½ hours turn the Red Wheel to 400 degrees. Drop the batter on the top of the meat and vegetables by tablespoonfuls. Spread so that it almost covers it, but leave a few openings. Bake at 400 degrees for ½ hour.

Yield: 6 servings.

MEAT SOUFFLÉ

Temperature, 325 degrees; Time, 1 hour

4 tablespoons butter	3 eggs
5 tablespoons flour	1½ cups left over meat
½ teaspoon salt	⅛ teaspoon pepper
1 cup milk	1/16 teaspoon cayenne

Melt the butter and add the flour and salt. Gradually add the milk, stirring constantly. Cool and add the beaten egg yolks, the chopped or ground meat, and the seasonings. Fold in, carefully, the stiffly-beaten egg whites and pour this mixture into a well-buttered baking dish. Place the dish in a pan containing 1 inch of boiling water and bake at 325 degrees for 1 hour.

Yield: 6 servings.

PEPPERS STUFFED WITH SAUSAGE

Temperature, 400 degrees; Time, 1 hour

6 peppers	1 teaspoon salt
½ pound sausage meat	1 cup tomatoes
2 cups cooked rice	½ cup boiling water

Wash the peppers and remove the seeds. Parboil for 5 minutes in water to cover over a surface burner. Remove from the water and fill them with the meat, cooked rice, salt, and strained tomatoes which have been mixed together. Place in a baking dish, add the boiling water and bake at 400 degrees for 1 hour. Bread crumbs may be used in place of the cooked rice, if desired.

Yield: 6 servings.

POT PIE

Temperature, 275 degrees; Time, 3 hours
then
Temperature, 350 degrees; Time, 20 minutes

2 pounds veal	2 cups potatoes
2 tablespoons fat	2 teaspoons salt
1 large onion	¼ teaspoon pepper
4 cups celery	4 cups boiling water
3 cups carrots	

For Dumplings

1 egg	1 teaspoon baking powder
⅓ cup milk	½ teaspoon salt
¾ cup flour	

Brown the sliced onion with the meat, which has been cut into 2-inch cubes, in the fat on the surface burner. Place it in a baking dish. Add the vegetables, which have been diced, the seasoning and the water. Cover and bake at 275 degrees for 3 hours.

While this mixture is baking prepare the dumplings. Beat the egg well, and add the milk. Sift the flour, baking powder and salt together. Add this to the egg mixture, stirring to make a smooth soft dough.

At the end of the baking period drop the dumpling dough on the meat and vegetable mixture by teaspoonfuls. Cover and return to the oven at 350 degrees for 20 minutes.

Yield: 6 servings.

SCALLOPED POTATOES AND HAM

Temperature, 400 degrees; Time, 1 hour

5 cups potatoes	2 teaspoons salt
4 tablespoons butter	1½ cups milk
4 tablespoons flour	1½-pound slice of ham

In a buttered baking dish put about one-third of the thinly sliced potatoes, butter, flour and salt. Prepare other layers in the same manner until all the ingredients are used. Add the milk. Cut the slice of ham around the edges to prevent curling and place on top of the potatoes. Bake at 400 degrees for 1 hour.

SALMON SOUFFLÉ

Temperature, 325 degrees; Time, 1 hour

4 tablespoons butter	1 cup milk
5 tablespoons flour	1 cup salmon
½ teaspoon salt	3 eggs

Melt the butter and add the flour and salt. Add the milk gradually, stirring constantly. Cool and add the flaked salmon and slightly-beaten egg yolks. Fold in the beaten whites and bake in a buttered baking dish set in 1 inch of boiling water at 325 degrees for 1 hour.

Yield: 6 servings.

SAUERKRAUT WITH PORK SHOULDER

Temperature, 275 degrees; Time, 3 or more hours

4 pounds sauerkraut   6 cups boiling water
3 pounds pork shoulder

Place half of the kraut in a baking dish. Add the meat and then the rest of the kraut. Pour enough boiling water over it to cover. Heat to boiling on surface burner. Cover, then place in the oven at 275 degrees for 3 or more hours. It may be served with dumplings if desired.

Yield: 6 servings.

SAUSAGE AND SPAGHETTI

Temperature, 400 degrees; Time, 45 minutes

2 cups spaghetti   ¼ teaspoon pepper
1 teaspoon salt   1½ cups canned tomatoes
      1 pound link sausage

Cook the broken spaghetti on a surface burner in enough boiling salted water to cover. When it is tender remove from the fire and drain. Put in a buttered baking dish and add the seasonings. Strain the tomatoes and add them. Brown the sausages in the oven at 400 degrees for 15 minutes while the spaghetti is boiling on top of the stove. When they are slightly brown put them on top of the spaghetti and tomato mixture. Bake at 400 degrees for ½ hour.

Yield: 6 servings.

SPAGHETTI AND TOMATOES

Temperature, 275 degrees; Time, 3 hours

1 cup spaghetti   ½ teaspoon curry powder
4 cups tomato pulp   1 cup cheese
1 teaspoon salt   2 tablespoons butter
⅛ teaspoon pepper

Mix the broken spaghetti, strained tomato pulp, salt, pepper and curry powder. Heat on the surface burner until it reaches the boiling point. Cover and place in the oven at 275 degrees for 2¾ hours. Then add the cheese, cut in pieces, and the butter. Continue baking for 15 minutes longer.

Yield: 6 servings.

SWEETBREAD PIE

Temperature, 450 degrees; Time, 25 minutes

1 pound sweetbreads	2 tablespoons parsley
12 soda crackers	2 teaspoons onion juice
4 tablespoons butter	½ green pepper
4 tablespoons flour	½ pimiento
1 teaspoon salt	½ teaspoon thyme
¼ teaspoon pepper	½ teaspoon marjoram
½ teaspoon paprika	3½ cups milk

Wash and parboil the sweetbreads in boiling water to cover for 5 minutes. Drain and remove the skin and divide into pieces. Butter a deep pie pan and fill with a layer of sweetbreads and crackers which have been broken into pieces. Chop the parsley, green pepper and pimiento very fine. Make a white sauce by adding the flour and seasonings to the melted butter. Then gradually add the milk, stirring constantly. Pour this over the sweetbreads and cover with pastry. See directions for Plain Pastry on p. 94. Bake at 450 degrees for 25 minutes.

Yield: 6 servings.

SWEETBREAD TIMBALES

Temperature, 400 degrees; Time, 25 minutes

½ pound sweetbreads	½ teaspoon paprika
4 eggs	1¾ cups milk
1 teaspoon salt	

Wash the sweetbreads in cold water. Parboil in boiling water for 5 minutes and remove the skin and veins from them. Pour cold water over them through a strainer. Chop and divide them evenly into 8 buttered custard cups. Beat the eggs and add the remaining ingredients. Pour this over the sweetbreads. Put the cups in a pan containing 1 inch of boiling water and bake at 400 degrees for 25 minutes. Garnish with broiled mushrooms.

Yield: 8 servings.

VEAL AND NOODLES

Temperature, 400 degrees; Time, 1 hour

or

Temperature, 275 degrees; Time, 3 hours*

2½ cups cold cubed veal	1½ teaspoons salt
2 cups celery	⅛ teaspoon pepper
1 green pepper	2½ cups liquid
¾ cup noodles	

Put the cubed left-over veal, sliced celery and pepper, broken uncooked noodles and seasonings in a casserole. Add the liquid which may be either gravy or cold water. If cold water is used add 1 bouillon cube and leave out ½ teaspoon of the salt. Cover and bake at either of the above temperatures. Use boiling water when baking at 400 degrees.

Yield: 6 servings.

VEAL AND RICE RING

Temperature, 350 degrees; Time, 1 hour

1 onion	1 tablespoon green pepper
2 tablespoons butter	2 teaspoons salt
2½ cups cooked rice	¼ teaspoon pepper
2½ cups previously cooked veal	1 egg
	1 cup milk

Brown the chopped onion in the butter. Mix the cooked rice and left-over ground veal and chopped pepper together. Add the rest of the ingredients and put in a well-buttered ring mold. Bake at 350 degrees for 1 hour.

Yield: 6 servings.

---

* This time and temperature is suitable for oven meals.

CHAPTER VIII

PIES AND TARTS

Pastry is a very variable product. The variability depends on several factors. The kind and quality of flour which is used will differ greatly; the size of the pieces of fat as they are distributed throughout the flour mixture will not always be the same; the consistency of fats will differ with the kind, and this may make a difference in the quality of the pastry; the amount of water absorbed will differ with different kinds of flour; the quality of the pastry is dependent to a certain extent on the temperature of the ingredients used and the way in which it is handled in the making; the amount of flour used on the board, and the number of times the dough is rolled; the strength used in rolling; the kind of material of which the pie dishes are made makes a difference in the browning—all of these factors will affect the finished product.

Pastry baked over the outside of an inverted pan will give a different result from that baked inside of the pan. When pastry is to be made into a shell and baked, then filled, it will bake quicker than when baked with an uncooked filling. This must be considered in the length of baking time and the temperature allowed.

There are several methods of mixing and on the one used for combining the ingredients will depend the desirability of the pastry.

PLAIN PASTRY

1½ cups flour ½ cup fat
½ teaspoon salt 4 or 5 tablespoons ice water

Sift the salt with the flour which has been sifted once before measuring. The fat should be worked into this, care being taken not to soften it more than is necessary. Use a fork or two knives to cut it in. When the fat has been worked in until it is of uniform size, add the cold water, slowly, until the mixture becomes a stiff dough which will hold together in one ball.

As much dough as is to be used for one crust should be placed on a slightly floured board. Then, with a floured rolling pin, roll the dough out into a thin sheet, keeping it as round as possible while rolling. It should be rolled out large enough to cover the pie dish which is to be used for the pie. If the crust is to be baked before filling put it over an inverted pie dish and trim the edges. Prick the crust with a fork to prevent it from forming blisters.

When a crust is to be made in which the filling is to be cooked as the crust bakes, line the pie dish with the pastry, prick it, and trim its edges. Then, fill the dish with the filling. If a top crust is wanted roll out more dough to a size that will cover the dish. Cut slashes in the dough to allow for the escape of steam, and trim the edges. Moisten the edge of the under crust with water and press the top crust to it.

* * * *

Pies

APPLE PIE

Temperature, 425 degrees; Time, 35 to 40 minutes

4 cups sliced apples ¼ teaspoon cinnamon
½ to ¾ cup sugar or nutmeg
1 teaspoon lemon juice ½ teaspoon salt
1 teaspoon grated lemon rind 2 tablespoons butter
1 tablespoon flour

Line a pie pan or glass dish with pastry. Wash, pare, core and slice the apples. Mix the sugar with the flour, add flavoring and salt. If the apples are dry add 1 or 2 tablespoons of water. Pour this apple mixture into the pie dish lined with pastry. Cut the butter into bits and put them on top of the apples. Moisten the edges of the under crust with water. Cut a few small gashes in the center of the upper crust. Then put it over the apples. Press the edges of the two crusts together; flute, and trim them. Bake at 425 degrees for 35 to 40 minutes.

If desired, ⅓ cup of grated cheese may be sprinkled over the top of the pie crust just before placing it in the oven.

Yield: One 9-inch pie.

BLACKBERRY PIE

Temperature, 425 degrees; Time, 35 to 40 minutes

3 cups blackberries   3 tablespoons flour
1 cup sugar

Put the washed berries, sugar and flour which have been mixed together into a pie dish lined with pastry. Cover with a top crust which has been gashed to allow for the escape of steam. Bake at 425 degrees for 35 to 40 minutes.

If canned berries are used, decrease the sugar to ½ or ¾ cup, and the flour to 2 tablespoons.

Yield: One 9-inch pie.

BLUEBERRY PIE

Temperature, 425 degrees; Time, 35 to 40 minutes

3 cups blueberries   3 tablespoons flour
¾ cup sugar

Wash the berries and add them to the sugar and flour which have been mixed together. Pour into a pastry lined pie dish. Cover with vented pastry. Press the edges together well; flute, and trim. Bake at 425 degrees for 35 to 40 minutes.

If canned berries are used decrease the sugar to ½ cup and the flour to 2 tablespoons.

Yield: One 9-inch pie.

BUTTERSCOTCH PIE

Temperature, 450 degrees for crust; Time, 12 to 15 minutes
then
Temperature, 300 degrees for meringue; Time, 15 to 20 minutes

1½ cups brown sugar 3 egg yolks
3 tablespoons water 4 tablespoons butter
3 cups milk ¾ teaspoon vanilla
7 tablespoons flour

Cook the brown sugar and water together until a syrup is formed. Put in the top of a double boiler and place over boiling water. Add some of the cold milk to the flour until it makes a thin, smooth paste. Combine the beaten egg yolks with the remainder of the milk, and add these two mixtures, one at a time to the syrup, stirring constantly. Let cook over a surface burner, stirring until it has thickened and is smooth. Add the butter and flavoring last. When the mixture has become thickened, put it in the baked pastry shell and cover with the following meringue:

Meringue

3 egg whites ½ teaspoon vanilla
¼ teaspoon salt ½ teaspoon almond extract
6 tablespoons sugar

Add the salt to the egg whites and beat until stiff. Fold the sugar gradually into them and add the flavoring. Spread this meringue on the top of the filling and place in the oven at 300 degrees for 15 to 20 minutes.

Yield: One 9-inch pie.

CHERRY PIE

Temperature, 425 degrees; Time, 35 to 40 minutes

4 cups cherries 3 tablespoons flour
1½ cups sugar 3 tablespoons cornstarch

After the seeds have been removed from the cherries add the sugar, flour, and cornstarch. Put into a pie dish lined with pastry and cover with the top crust in which openings have been cut. Moisten the edges of the crust; press together; flute and trim. Bake at 425 degrees for 35 to 40 minutes.

If canned cherries are used decrease the sugar to 1 cup; the cornstarch to 2 tablespoons, and the flour to 2 tablespoons.

Yield: One 9-inch pie.

CHOCOLATE PIE

Temperature, 450 degrees for crust; Time, 12 to 15 minutes
then
Temperature, 300 degrees for meringue; Time, 15 to 20 minutes

3 eggs	4 tablespoons flour
1 cup sugar	2 tablespoons cornstarch
3 cups milk	2 ounces chocolate
	1 teaspoon vanilla

Beat the egg yolks and add the sugar. Make a thin smooth paste by adding a little of the milk to the flour and cornstarch. Scald the remainder of the milk and stir a little of it into each of the above mixtures. Then slowly stir them into the scalded milk. Melt the chocolate slowly over hot water and add to the custard mixture. Cook and stir until thickened. Add the flavoring and pour into a baked pastry shell. Cover with a meringue (see p. 96). Bake the meringue at 300 degrees for 15 to 20 minutes.

Yield: One 9-inch pie.

CRANBERRY PIE

Temperature, 425 degrees; Time, 35 to 40 minutes

2 apples	½ cup water
2 cups cranberries	1¼ cups sugar

Peel and slice the apples as for pie and add to the washed cranberries. Add the water and cook until the skins of the berries break. Add the sugar and pour into a pie dish lined with pastry. Put strips of pastry over the top in criss cross fashion and bake at 425 degrees for 35 to 40 minutes.

Yield: One 9-inch pie.

CREAM PIE

Temperature, 450 degrees for crust; Time, 12 to 15 minutes
then
Temperature, 300 degrees for meringue; Time, 15 to 20 minutes

3 cups milk	½ cup sugar
4 tablespoons flour	⅛ teaspoon salt
2 tablespoons cornstarch	3 tablespoons butter
3 eggs	1 teaspoon vanilla

Mix the flour and cornstarch with ⅓ cup of the cold milk to a thin smooth paste. Then scald the remaining milk. Beat the egg yolks, add the sugar and salt. Add a small amount of the scalded milk to the flour paste and some to the egg and sugar mixture. Pour each mixture slowly into the scalded milk. Stir together to prevent lumping and cook until thick. Remove from the fire, add the butter and flavoring. Pour into a well-baked pastry shell. Cover with a meringue (see p. 96) and brown at 300 degrees for 15 to 20 minutes.

Add 1 cup of shredded moist cocoanut to the custard for variation.

Yield: One 9-inch pie.

CRUMB PIE

Temperature, 375 degrees; Time, 40 minutes

¾ cup sugar	½ cup molasses
1¾ cups flour	¼ cup boiling water
½ cup butter	½ teaspoon soda
1 egg	

Mix the sugar, flour and butter together. Save out ½ cup of this mixture for the crumbs to be used on the top of the pies. Beat the egg and add the molasses and boiling water in which the soda has been dissolved. Add to the sugar mixture. Pour into two unbaked pastry shells. Sprinkle the crumbs over the top and bake at 375 degrees for 40 minutes.

Yield: Two 9-inch pies.

CUSTARD PIE

Temperature, 450 degrees; Time, 10 minutes
then
Temperature, 325 degrees; Time, 30 minutes

3 cups milk	¼ teaspoon salt
3 eggs	1 teaspoon vanilla
½ cup sugar	Few gratings of nutmeg, if desired

Roll the pastry and place it on the pie dish. Be sure that it is flat to the dish so that no air bubbles are beneath. Place it in the refrigerator for 1 hour. Scald the milk. Beat the eggs slightly. Add the sugar, salt, and vanilla. Add the scalded milk and pour this mixture into the chilled crust. Bake at 450 degrees for 10 minutes, then 325 degrees for 30 minutes.

Yield: One 9-inch pie.

LEMON MERINGUE PIE

Temperature, 450 degrees for crust; Time, 12 to 15 minutes
then
Temperature, 300 degrees for meringue; Time, 15 to 20 minutes

6 tablespoons flour	1 lemon rind, grated
3 tablespoons cornstarch	½ cup lemon juice
1 cup sugar	1 tablespoon butter
3 cups boiling water	¼ teaspoon salt
3 egg yolks	

Mix the flour, cornstarch and sugar together. Add the boiling water, stirring while adding. Stir and cook over a low flame for 15 minutes. Beat the egg yolks slightly and add part of the hot mixture to them. Mix well and return it to the remainder of the sugar and starch mixture. Stir and cook over a low flame until the egg yolks are thickened. Remove from the fire, add the lemon rind and juice, butter and salt, and mix well. Pour into the baked pastry shell, and cover with a meringue (see p. 96).

Yield: One 9-inch pie.

PEACH PIE

Temperature, 425 degrees; Time, 35 to 40 minutes

3½ cups peaches   ⅔ cup sugar
3 tablespoons flour   ⅛ teaspoon salt

Wash the peaches, remove the skins, slice and measure. Put them together with the flour, sugar and salt, into a pie dish lined with pastry. Cover with a top crust in which cuts have been made to allow for the escape of the steam. Press the edges of the crusts together, flute, and trim. Bake at 425 degrees for 35 to 40 minutes.

Yield: One 9-inch pie.

PRUNE PIE

Temperature, 425 degrees; Time, 35 to 40 minutes

3 cups prunes   2 tablespoons lemon juice
½ cup sugar   1 teaspoon cinnamon

Remove the pits from the previously cooked prunes and cut in quarters. Mix the sugar, prunes, lemon juice and cinnamon together. Pour into a pie dish lined with pastry. Cut some pastry into strips and put them over the top in criss cross fashion. Bake at 425 degrees for 35 to 40 minutes.

Yield: One 9-inch pie.

PUMPKIN or SQUASH PIE

Temperature, 450 degrees; Time, 10 minutes
then
Temperature, 325 degrees; Time, 30 minutes

2 tablespoons butter   ⅜ teaspoon cinnamon
½ cup sugar   ½ teaspoon salt
3 eggs   1½ cups squash or pumpkin
⅜ teaspoon ginger   1½ cups milk
⅜ teaspoon cloves

Roll the pastry and place it on the pie dish. Be sure that it is flat to the dish so that no air bubbles are beneath. Place it in the refrigerator to chill.

Melt the butter, add the sugar and well beaten eggs. Add the spices and salt. Then add the cup of hot cooked and mashed squash or pumpkin. Add the scalded milk and bake at 450 degrees for 10 minutes, then 325 degrees for 30 minutes.

Yield: One 9 inch pie.

RASPBERRY PIE

(Black or Red)

Temperature, 425 degrees; Time, 35 to 40 minutes

3 cups raspberries   ¾ cup sugar
3 tablespoons flour

Wash the berries and drain them. Add the flour and sugar. Pour into a pie dish lined with pastry. Cover with a crust in which openings have been made. Press the edges together, flute, and trim. Bake at 425 degrees for 35 to 40 minutes.

If canned berries are used decrease the sugar to ½ cup, and the flour to 2 tablespoons.

Yield: One 9-inch pie.

RHUBARB PIE

Temperature, 425 degrees; Time, 35 to 40 minutes

3½ cups rhubarb   1¼ cups sugar
6 tablespoons flour   1 egg

Cut the rhubarb into pieces and measure. Mix in the flour, sugar and egg which has been beaten slightly. Put in a pie dish lined with pastry and cover with a top crust in which openings have been made. Press the edges together, flute, and trim. Bake at 425 degrees for 35 to 40 minutes.

Yield: One 9-inch pie.

Tarts

Tarts and fanchonettes make pleasing varieties of an age-old dessert. They may be used at the end of a meal to take the place of the proverbial pie.

PLAIN PASTRY

1 cup pastry flour	⅓ cup butter
⅓ teaspoon salt	3 tablespoons ice water

Measure the flour after sifting once. Sift again with the salt. Cut in the butter and add enough ice water to make a stiff dough. The dough may be baked over small pans made expressly for the purpose, or muffin pans may be used. If the filling is to be baked in the pastry muffin pans will not be satisfactory.

Yield: 6 tart shells.

APPLE TARTS

Temperature, 400 degrees; Time, 35 minutes

3 cups apples	2 tablespoons flour
⅓ cup sugar	½ teaspoon cinnamon
⅓ teaspoon salt	½ pint cream

Mix the sliced apples with the sugar, salt, flour and cinnamon. Put into small pastry lined tart tins. Pour in enough cream to almost cover. Strips of pastry may be put across the top, if desired, or the tarts can be baked with no covering. Bake at 400 degrees for 35 minutes.

Yield: 6 tarts.

APRICOT TARTS

Temperature, 450 degrees; Time, 12 to 15 minutes

½ pound dried apricots	½ cup sugar
2 cups water	

Soak the apricots over night in the water, and cook slowly the next day until tender. These can be cooked at 350 degrees for 35 minutes if the oven is being used at this temperature for other foods. Rub them through a sieve.

Add the sugar to the pulp and cook over a surface burner for a few minutes. This makes 2 cups of filling. Fill tart shells which have been previously baked at 450 degrees for 12 to 15 minutes. They may be served plain or topped with a small amount of whipped cream.

Yield: 6 tarts.

BUTTERSCOTCH TARTS

Temperature, 450 degrees; Time, 12 to 15 minutes
then
Temperature, 300 degrees; Time, 15 to 20 minutes

1 cup brown sugar	2 cups milk
2 tablespoons water	2 egg yolks
3 tablespoons butter	½ teaspoon lemon juice
5 tablespoons flour	⅛ teaspoon almond extract
¼ teaspoon salt	2 egg whites

Cook the sugar, water and butter to a rich syrup. Mix the flour, salt and part of the milk to a paste. Beat the egg yolks and add the remaining milk to them. Add both mixtures slowly to the syrup, stirring constantly to avoid lumps, and cook until thickened. Remove from the fire and add the flavoring. Pour into tart shells baked at 450 degrees for 12 to 15 minutes.

Use 2 egg whites, stiffly beaten for a meringue (see p. 63) to spread over the top of the tarts. Bake at 300 degrees for 15 to 20 minutes.

Yield: 6 tarts.

CRANBERRY TARTS

Temperature, 425 degrees; Time, 30 to 35 minutes

1½ cups cranberries	1 cup sugar
½ cup raisins	¼ teaspoon salt
½ cup nut meats	

Put all the ingredients except the sugar and salt through the coarse grinder of the food chopper. Add the sugar and salt and put into tart pans lined with unbaked pastry. Cut some pastry into strips and arrange criss cross fashion over the tops. Bake at 425 degrees for 30 to 35 minutes.

Yield: 6 tarts.

LEMON TARTS

Temperature, 450 degrees; Time, 12 to 15 minutes
then
Temperature, 300 degrees; Time, 15 to 20 minutes

4 tablespoons cornstarch
1 cup sugar
¼ teaspoon salt
1 cup boiling water
2 egg yolks

6 tablespoons lemon juice
1 lemon rind, grated
1 tablespoon butter
2 egg whites

Mix the cornstarch, sugar and salt. Add the boiling water slowly, stirring constantly. Stir and cook over a slow fire until thickened. Stir in the beaten egg yolks and remove from the fire. Then add the lemon juice, rind and the butter. Stir these in well. Pour into tart shells which have been baked at 450 degrees for 12 to 15 minutes. Spread with a meringue made of the beaten egg whites (see p. 63). Bake at 300 degrees for 15 to 20 minutes.

Yield: 5 tarts.

LEMON SPONGE TARTS

Temperature, 425 degrees; Time, 10 minutes
then
Temperature, 325 degrees; Time, 25 minutes

2 tablespoons flour
1 cup sugar
2 egg yolks
5 tablespoons lemon juice

1 lemon rind, grated
1 cup milk
¼ teaspoon salt
2 egg whites

Mix the flour and sugar together. Add the beaten egg yolks with the lemon juice and grated rind. Then add the milk and the egg whites which have been beaten with the salt. Pour into unbaked individual pastry shells and bake at 425 degrees for 10 minutes, then 325 degrees for 25 minutes.

Yield: 6 tarts.

PEACH FANCHONETTES

Temperature, 425 degrees; Time, 15 minutes
then
Temperature, 300 degrees; Time, 15 to 20 minutes

6 halves of peaches
1 egg yolk
¼ cup cream

½ cup sugar
¼ teaspoon salt

Line the tart pans with pastry. Fill each with half of a large peach cut side down. Mix the egg yolk, cream, sugar and salt, and pour over the fruit. Bake at 425 degrees for 15 minutes. Spread with a meringue (see p. 63) and bake. Any other fruit, either fresh or canned, may be used for this recipe.

Yield: 6 tarts.

PECAN FANCHONETTES

Temperature, 425 degrees; Time, 15 minutes
then
Temperature, 325 degrees; Time, 12 minutes

1 egg
¼ cup milk
1 cup brown sugar
1 teaspoon butter

½ cup pecan meats
⅛ teaspoon salt
½ teaspoon vanilla

Beat the whole egg and add the remaining ingredients. Mix thoroughly. Pour into tart pans lined with unbaked pastry. Bake at 425 degrees for 15 minutes, then 325 degrees for 12 minutes.

If desired, 2 egg yolks may be used in the custard and the whites reserved for a meringue. If the meringue is used bake the pastry and filling at 425 degrees for 15 minutes. Add the meringue and turn the Red Wheel to 300 degrees for 15 to 20 minutes to finish baking the tarts and to brown the meringue.

Yield: 6 tarts.

CHAPTER IX

POULTRY

The most commonly used varieties of poultry are chicken, turkey, duck and goose. The last two are entirely dark meated and, when compared with chicken or turkey, have a slightly gamy flavor.

The same general rule holds true for cooking poultry as for meats. For roasting and baking it should be browned in a hot oven, then cooked through uniformly at a reduced temperature. It should be baked or roasted covered unless very young and tender, in which case it may be left uncovered.

* * * *

Chicken

BAKED CHICKEN

Temperature, 400 degrees; Time, 2 hours

or

Temperature, 275 degrees; Time, 3 hours*

5-pound stewing chicken	⅛ teaspoon pepper
2 tablespoons flour	1 teaspoon salt
2 tablespoons butter	1 teaspoon dried parsley

Have the chicken cleaned, dressed, and cut for stewing. Place it in a casserole and spread 2 tablespoons of flour over the top. Then put the 2 tablespoons of melted butter, pepper, salt and dried parsley over the chicken. Cover and bake at either of the above temperatures. If possible, uncover the chicken for the last ½ hour to allow for browning.

---

* This time and temperature is suitable for oven meals.

MARYLAND CHICKEN

Temperature, 350 degrees; Time, 1½ to 2 hours
or
Temperature, 275 degrees; Time, 3 hours*

4½ to 5-pound chicken,   1½ cups crumbs
    1 year old   1 egg
1½ teaspoons salt   ½ cup milk
⅛ teaspoon pepper   ½ cup boiling water

Singe the chicken and cut it into pieces. Wash thoroughly.
Add the salt and pepper to the fine bread or cracker crumbs.
Beat the egg and add the milk. Dip the pieces of chicken into
the egg and milk mixture, then into the crumbs. Repeat this
process and brown the chicken in deep fat heated to a temperature
of 375 degrees Fahrenheit, or in a frying pan in 4 tablespoons of
melted fat. Place in a baking dish and add ½ cup of boiling
water. Cover and bake at either of the above temperatures.

ROAST CHICKEN

Temperature, 500 degrees for searing; Time, 20 minutes
then
Temperature, 275 degrees; Time, 28 to 30 minutes per pound

5-pound roasting chicken   1 teaspoon salt
1 quart bread crumbs   ⅛ teaspoon pepper
4 tablespoons butter   ¼ cup boiling water
1 onion

Remove the pin feathers and oil bag from the dressed chicken.
Singe over a gas flame. Wash well both inside and out, being
sure the lungs and all entrails have been removed. Stuff the
chicken with a stuffing made by mixing the crumbs, melted butter,
chopped onion, salt, pepper and other seasonings such as bay
leaf, or poultry seasoning if desired. Sew through the skin and
truss.

To truss a chicken tie or skewer the wings and legs close to
the body to prevent them from drying out while baking. Place
on a rack in a roaster and sear at 500 degrees for 20 minutes.
Add ¼ cup of boiling water, cover and bake at 275 degrees for
28 to 30 minutes per pound.

---

* This time and temperature is suitable for oven meals.

STEWED CHICKEN WITH DROP BISCUITS AND GRAVY

Temperature, 275 degrees; Time, 3 hours

then

Temperature, 475 degrees for biscuits; Time 15 to 20 minutes

Cut a 3½ or 4-pound chicken for stewing. Place the pieces on a rack in a roaster. Sprinkle 1 tablespoon of salt over it. Pour 2 cups of boiling water in the bottom of the pan and cover. If the cover has a valve, open it. Place in the oven at 275 degrees for 3 hours.

When the baking period is completed, remove the pan from the oven and pour the broth from the pan, but save it for the gravy.

Have ready a biscuit mixture made as follows:

2 cups flour	4 tablespoons fat
4 teaspoons baking powder	¾ cup milk
1 teaspoon salt	

Mix and sift the flour, baking powder and salt. Work in the fat. Add the milk, mixing it with the other ingredients by cutting the mixture with a knife. Drop a tablespoon of the dough on top of each piece of chicken. Place the chicken and biscuit mixture in the oven at 475 degrees and bake uncovered for 15 to 20 minutes.

While the biscuits are baking, prepare a gravy, using the broth drained from the chicken. Use the following ingredients and method:

6 tablespoons flour	6 tablespoons butter
½ teaspoon salt	broth
⅛ teaspoon pepper	

In a sauce pan mix the flour, salt, pepper and butter. Add the hot broth and enough water to make 3 cups of liquid. Stir and cook on the surface burner until the mixture reaches the boiling point. Serve hot over the chicken and biscuit.

Yield: 6 servings.

Goose

ROAST GOOSE

Temperature, 500 degrees for searing; Time, 20 to 30 minutes
then
Temperature, 275 degrees; Time, 3 hours

Select a goose that is not more than 1 year old weighing about
8 or 10 pounds. Singe and remove the pin feathers. Clean by
drawing as though it were any other kind of fowl. Wipe out
the inside cavity carefully and sprinkle with salt. Cut off the
neck, leaving only 1 inch of the skin, which should be tied shut
to prevent the stuffing from coming out during baking. Cut off
the wings of the goose, leaving only the first joint.

Stuffing

½ cup onion   1 teaspoon salt
3 tablespoons fat   ⅛ teaspoon pepper
1½ quarts stale bread   1 egg
1½ cups celery

The seasonings may be changed to suit individual or family
tastes. Sometimes a stuffing of mashed potatoes is preferred.
This is then mixed with onion, chopped parsley, fine bread crumbs,
eggs and butter. Nuts may be added to either kind of dressing.

Brown the sliced onion in the fat melted in a frying pan over
a surface burner. Then add the cubed bread which has been
soaked in cold water and squeezed dry between the hands. When
slightly brown and dry remove from the fire and add the remaining ingredients. The giblets may be chopped and added to the
stuffing or saved for the gravy. Stuff the goose, place on a rack
in a roaster, and sear at 500 degrees for 20 to 30 minutes. Add
the cleaned giblets and 1 cup of boiling water. Then reduce the
oven temperature to 275 degrees and let bake uncovered for 3
hours. If the goose is old or tough cover it and let bake for the
given length of time. Prepare a Giblet Gravy according to the
directions given on p. 110.

Turkey

ROAST TURKEY

Temperature, 500 degrees for searing; Time, 20 to 30 minutes
then
Temperature, 275 degrees; Time, 15 to 20 minutes per pound

Select a young turkey. If not already removed, cut off the head and feet. Loosen the skin from the neck, push the skin back and cut off the neck close to the body. Remove the pin feathers and cut the oil bag from the tail. Remove the internal parts unless this has been done at the time the poultry was purchased. Cut the giblets from the entrails. Wash the turkey inside and out. Wash the giblets. Prepare a stuffing, using the following ingredients:

2 quarts bread crumbs	¼ teaspoon pepper
4 teaspoons salt	½ cup butter

Mix the stale crumbs and seasoning. Melt the butter and add the seasoned crumbs. Two teaspoons of ground sage may be added if desired. Stir and heat until the crumbs are slightly browned. In order that the wings and legs may not become drier than the other parts of the turkey, they should be tied or skewered (trussed) close to the body of the turkey.

Place the turkey on a rack in a roaster. Sear at 500 degrees for 20 to 30 minutes. Then remove it from the oven and sprinkle with at least 1 tablespoon of salt, and add 1½ cups of boiling water. Place the giblets and neck at the edge of the rack so they come in contact with the water. Cover the pan and place in the oven at 275 degrees for 15 to 20 minutes per pound. The smaller the turkey the longer the time per pound for roasting.

Giblet Gravy

8 tablespoons turkey fat or butter	1 cup water
	Chopped giblets
½ cup flour	½ teaspoon pepper
Turkey broth	1 teaspoon salt

Skim the fat from the broth around the turkey, or use butter. Place in a sauce pan and add the flour. Stir and cook over a flame until the mixture is browned. Then add the turkey broth and boiling water. Stir and cook until the mixture is thickened. Chop the giblets and add them to the gravy together with the pepper and salt.

CHAPTER X

SAUCES

Dessert Sauces

ANISE SAUCE

½ cup butter   1 egg
1 cup powdered sugar   2 drops anise flavoring

Cream the butter and add the sugar gradually. Add the well-beaten egg and cook over the hot water, stirring constantly, until the egg is cooked. Remove from the fire, and add the flavoring.

Yield: 6 servings.

APRICOT SAUCE

½ pound dried apricots   6 tablespoons water
⅓ cup sugar   1 tablespoon lemon juice

Soak the apricots and cook slowly until tender. Put through a strainer. This amount of dried fruit will yield about ¾ cup of pulp when strained. Add the sugar and water to this pulp, and cook slowly for about 5 minutes. Add the lemon juice and serve either hot or cold. If the sauce thickens when cold and is desired thinner, add a tablespoon more of water and mix thoroughly.

Yield: 6 servings.

BUTTERSCOTCH SAUCE

1½ cups brown sugar   ¾ cup cream
⅔ cup white corn syrup   ⅓ cup pecan meats
4 tablespoons butter   ⅛ teaspoon salt

Cook the sugar, syrup and butter together until it reaches 230 degrees Fahrenheit, or when a soft ball forms when dropped in cold water. Then add the thin cream, very slowly, stirring constantly. Add the nut meats and salt. Serve either hot or cold.

Yield: 6 servings.

CHERRY SAUCE

1½ cups cherry juice   2 teaspoons cornstarch

Heat the juice from the canned cherries or fresh sour cherries, and add it slowly to the cornstarch which has been mixed to a thin paste with a little of the cold cherry juice. If fresh sour cherries are used, add sugar to suit the taste. Cook over a surface burner until it is thickened slightly, stirring constantly to avoid lumps.

Yield: 6 servings.

CHOCOLATE SAUCE

(No. 1)

2 ounces chocolate   2 tablespoons butter
2 cups sugar   1 teaspoon vanilla
¾ cup water

Cut the chocolate into small pieces and put it with the sugar and water into a sauce pan. Cook on the surface burner, stirring until the sugar is dissolved. Cook the mixture until it spins a thread (about 228 degrees Fahrenheit). Remove from the fire, add the butter, and cool. When slightly cool add the vanilla and stir to mix well.

(No. 2)

1½ tablespoons cornstarch   2 eggs
1 pint milk   ⅔ cup sugar
2 ounces chocolate   1 teaspoon vanilla

Mix the cornstarch with a little cold milk, then add to the rest of the milk which has been scalded. Cook in a double boiler until slightly thickened, then add the grated chocolate which has been melted. Add the sugar to the beaten eggs. Pour this into the cooked mixture. Stir and cook for 1 minute. Let cool, add the vanilla and serve.

Yield: 5 servings.

CURRANT HARD SAUCE

¼ cup butter   ⅔ cup currant jelly
1 cup powdered sugar

Cream the butter and add the sugar gradually. Beat the jelly with a silver fork and add to the butter and sugar mixture. Beat until well mixed.

Yield: 5 servings.

CUSTARD SAUCE

1½ cups milk   ⅛ teaspoon salt
¼ cup sugar   ½ teaspoon vanilla
2 eggs

Heat the milk over hot water. Mix the sugar with the eggs which have been well beaten. Add this slowly to the scalded milk, stirring constantly until thickened. Remove from the fire and add the salt and vanilla. Chill.

Yield: 6 servings.

FOAMY SAUCE

2 tablespoons butter   3 tablespoons boiling water
⅓ cup powdered sugar   1 tablespoon vanilla or
2 eggs   sherry flavoring

Cream the butter and add the sugar, then the well-beaten egg yolks. Next fold in the well-beaten egg whites, and the boiling water. Cook in a double boiler until thick. Cool and add the flavoring.

Yield: 6 servings.

HARD SAUCE

6 tablespoons butter   1½ teaspoons vanilla or
1½ cups powdered sugar   sherry flavoring

Cream the butter well. Then add the sugar gradually. Lastly add the flavoring.

Yield: 6 servings.

LEMON SAUCE

1 cup sugar   4 tablespoons butter
2 tablespoons cornstarch   3 tablespoons lemon juice
2 cups boiling water   ¼ teaspoon salt

Mix the sugar and cornstarch together. Add the water gradually, stirring constantly. Boil for 5 minutes. Then remove from the fire and add the butter, lemon juice and salt.

Yield: 6 servings.

ORANGE SAUCE

1 cup cold water   2 tablespoons butter
2 tablespoons cornstarch   1 cup sugar
¼ teaspoon salt   2 eggs
1 orange rind, grated   1 cup orange juice
     2 tablespoons lemon juice

Mix the water, cornstarch, salt and grated orange rind well. Stir and cook on a surface burner for 5 minutes. Add the butter, sugar and beaten egg yolks and mix thoroughly. Place in a sauce pan and put this on an asbestos mat over the burner. Stir and cook the sauce until the egg yolks are thickened. Remove from the fire and beat the egg whites until stiff. Then fold them into the hot mixture. Add the orange and lemon juices and mix well.

Yield: 6 servings.

Salad Dressings

FRENCH DRESSING

½ teaspoon onion juice
¼ teaspoon pepper
¾ teaspoon salt
1 teaspoon paprika

¾ cup olive oil
2 tablespoons vinegar
2 tablespoons lemon juice

Mix the seasonings together, and add the oil. Beat and then pour the vinegar and lemon juice slowly on these ingredients, beating until the dressing is thickened.

Yield: ½ pint.

TOMATO FRENCH DRESSING

⅛ clove garlic
2 tablespoons catsup
1 teaspoon salt
½ teaspoon pepper
½ teaspoon mustard

½ teaspoon sugar
¾ cup olive oil
2½ tablespoons vinegar or
    lemon juice

Rub the mixing bowl with the clove of garlic, add the seasonings. Slowly add the oil, beating while adding. It is best to have the oil very cold before using. Then beat in the vinegar or lemon juice.

Yield: ½ pint.

MAYONNAISE

2 egg yolks
2 teaspoons mustard
1 teaspoon salt
½ teaspoon pepper

½ teaspoon paprika
2 cups olive oil
4 tablespoons vinegar

Beat the egg yolks until they are thick and lemon colored. Add the dry ingredients, then slowly add 1½ cups of olive oil, beating while slowly pouring it into the egg yolks. Then add the vinegar, slowly, beating constantly. Slowly pour in the remainder of the oil. Do not stop beating for very long during the making of the Mayonnaise.

Yield: 1 pint.

Meat, Fish, and Vegetable Sauces

BECHAMEL SAUCE

1½ cups meat stock
1 slice of onion
Bit of bay leaf
6 peppercorns
½ teaspoon chopped parsley
¼ cup butter

¼ cup flour
1 cup scalded milk
½ teaspoon salt
⅛ teaspoon pepper
¼ teaspoon paprika

Cook the meat stock with the onion, bay leaf, peppercorns and parsley for 20 minutes. Then strain. Melt the butter and add the flour. Then gradually add the hot stock mixture and the scalded milk. Add the seasonings, and cook over a surface burner for about 20 minutes, stirring constantly.

BROWN SAUCE

2 tablespoons flour
2 tablespoons butter
1 teaspoon onion juice

1 cup vegetable or meat stock
½ teaspoon salt
⅛ teaspoon pepper

Brown the flour by heating slowly over a low flame, stirring constantly. Add the butter and cream well. Then add the onion juice and the stock. Stir and cook until smooth. Add the seasonings and serve hot.

CURRANT MINT SAUCE

1 glass currant jelly
3 tablespoons chopped mint

½ orange rind

Whip the jelly with a silver fork and add the chopped mint and grated orange rind. Mix well and serve.

HOLLANDAISE SAUCE

½ cup butter
2 egg yolks
1 tablespoon lemon juice

⅓ teaspoon salt
¼ teaspoon paprika
Dash of cayenne

Wash the butter in ice-cold water until it is waxy. Divide it into 3 equal parts and put ⅓ in the top of a small double boiler with the egg yolks and lemon juice. Put into the bottom part of the double boiler which contains water kept just below the boiling temperature. Stir vigorously until the mixture thickens. Add the second piece of butter; stir again, and when thick and smooth add the last piece. Remove from the hot water and add the seasonings.

HORSERADISH SAUCE

¼ cup whipping cream   ¼ teaspoon salt
3 tablespoons horseradish

Whip the cream until stiff and add the horseradish. More or less horseradish may be used, depending on its sharpness. If it is dry add 1 teaspoon of vinegar or lemon juice to the mixture before serving. Add the salt and stir well to blend.

MAÎTRE D'HÔTEL BUTTER

¼ cup butter   ½ tablespoon parsley
½ teaspoon salt   ¼ teaspoon paprika
⅛ teaspoon pepper   ¾ teaspoon lemon juice

Put the butter in a bowl and, with a small wooden spoon work it until it is creamy. Add the salt, pepper, parsley and paprika. Then add the lemon juice very slowly, stirring while adding.

MUSHROOM SAUCE

3 tablespoons butter   1½ cups milk
1½ cups small mushrooms   ½ teaspoon salt
3 tablespoons flour   ⅛ teaspoon pepper

Brown the butter and mushrooms together in a saucepan. Add the flour and stir to mix well. Then slowly add the scalded milk. Stir to keep smooth, and cook until thickened. Add the salt and pepper and serve.

MUSTARD SAUCE

2 tablespoons butter
2 tablespoons flour
1 cup hot vegetable stock
½ teaspoon salt
¼ teaspoon pepper
1 teaspoon mustard
2 tablespoons lemon juice
  or weak vinegar

Brown the butter well, add the flour and brown it. Add the stock. Stir and cook until smooth. Add the seasonings which have been mixed with the lemon juice or vinegar. Serve with Baked Ham.

TOMATO SAUCE

2 cups strained tomatoes
3 slices onion
8 peppercorns
1 bay leaf
2 cloves
2 tablespoons butter
2 tablespoons flour
1 tablespoon sugar
½ teaspoon salt

Cook the first five ingredients together for 15 minutes. Then remove from the fire and strain. Heat the butter and add the flour. Then add the strained tomato mixture. Cook and stir until thickened. Add the sugar and salt and serve.

VINAIGRETTE SAUCE

1 teaspoon salt
¼ teaspoon paprika
1 teaspoon pepper
1 tablespoon tarragon
  vinegar
2 tablespoons cider vinegar
6 tablespoons olive oil
1 teaspoon chopped chives
1 tablespoon chopped
  pickles
1 tablespoon chopped
  green pepper
1 teaspoon chopped
  parsley
Dash of cayenne

Mix the ingredients in the order given. Beat well to blend and serve.

CHAPTER XI

SOUPS

There are two general classes of soups. One has a foundation of milk flavored with vegetables and otherwise well seasoned. The other is made by extracting the juices and flavor from meat or fish and adding vegetables and other seasonings for additional flavor.

Soups may be used either as the main dish at the meal or as an appetizer to serve at the beginning of a meal. When used as the main dish a cream soup or chowder is used, or vegetables and bits of meat are left in the broth which is slightly thickened by rice, barley, noodles, or some starchy vegetable. When used as an appetizer at the beginning of the meal, the fat is removed from it and the soup is usually clear.

When meat is used as a base for soup stock the juices should be extracted as they contain most of the flavoring. The meat should be placed in cold water and then brought to the boiling point and simmered slowly for a long period of time. This may be accomplished in a Lorain Controlled Oven if desired.

BEAN SOUP

1 pound beans	1 pound end of ham
3 cups water	2 tablespoons butter
2 teaspoons salt	2 tablespoons flour
½ teaspoon pepper	

Soak any kind of dried beans over night. The next morning drain them. Put them in a soup kettle with the cold water, salt, pepper and end of ham which has been skinned. Onion juice or other seasoning may be added. Cover and simmer about 2 hours. Then strain. Cream the butter and flour together. Add 1 cup of the warm soup stock slowly, stirring constantly. Then pour this slowly into the soup and stir until it reaches the boiling point to cook the flour. If prepared in the oven, bring to a boil and simmer at 275 degrees for 3 hours.

Yield: 6 servings.

BOUILLON

4 pounds soup meat (including bone)
1 small onion
1 tablespoon salt
¼ teaspoon pepper
½ cup carrots
½ cup potatoes
½ cup celery
5 cups water

Cut the meat from the bone and into cubes of about an inch. Put these and the bone in a large pan and sear in a small amount of fat. Add the seasonings, diced vegetables and the cold water. Simmer gently for 4 or 5 hours or bring to boiling point, then simmer in the oven at 275 degrees for 3 hours.

This soup should be made a day before it is wanted and kept in a cool place. Then any excess fat can be easily skimmed off, as it will have hardened on the top. If it is not possible to let the soup stand over night, the fat can be skimmed off with a spoon when hot if great care is taken. If the soup is desired free from all fat, it can be poured over some cracked ice after skimming and the fat particles will harden and adhere to the ice. Any fat remaining after this treatment can be taken off by passing a clean blotting paper through the surface of the soup. The blotting paper will absorb the fat.

If a perfectly clear soup is desired, the vegetables should be strained from the liquid and the white of an egg slightly beaten with the washed and crushed shell added to the cool soup. Place it over the fire and stir constantly until it has boiled several minutes. Remove from the fire and strain through a very fine clean cheese cloth. This clear broth can then be reheated and served hot. For a more filling soup the vegetables may be left in.

Yield: 6 servings.

CHICKEN NOODLE SOUP

1 cup celery
1 onion
Bones from left-over roast
   chicken
10 cups water

1 tablespoon salt
½ teaspoon pepper
1½ cups narrow egg
   noodles

Cut the celery and onion into small pieces. Put all of the ingredients except the noodles in a pan. Bring to the boiling point. Then cover and simmer gently for about 2 hours. Strain and again bring to the boiling point. Add the noodles, cover, and cook for 15 to 20 minutes, or simmer in the oven for 2½ hours at 275 degrees. Strain and proceed as above.

Yield: 6 servings.

CORN CHOWDER

3 ounces salt pork
1½ onions
2¼ cups boiling water
1 quart diced potatoes
1½ quarts corn pulp

¾ tablespoon salt
¾ teaspoon pepper
¾ teaspoon paprika
3 tablespoons butter
3 cups milk

Brown the cubes of salt pork in the pan to be used. Add the diced onions and brown. Then add the boiling water, diced potatoes, corn (fresh or canned) and the seasonings. Cover and cook until the corn and potatoes are tender (about ½ hour) or place in the oven at 350 degrees for 1¼ hours. At the end of this time add the butter and scalded milk. Serve at once.

Yield: 6 servings.

OXTAIL SOUP

2 tablespoons fat	3 cloves
1 onion	¼ teaspoon pepper
1 oxtail	½ cup celery
2 quarts cold water	½ cup carrots
3 teaspoons salt	3 tablespoons barley

Melt the fat and add the chopped onion and oxtail, cut in pieces. Brown. Add the remaining ingredients. The celery and carrots should be diced or cut fine. Cover and simmer gently for 2 hours, or bring to a boil and place in the oven at 275 degrees for 3 hours.

For clear soup follow the directions for clearing as given on p. 120 under Bouillon.

Yield: 6 servings.

SPLIT PEA SOUP

2 cups peas	2 teaspoons salt
2 quarts water	⅛ teaspoon pepper
1 pound end of ham	2 tablespoons butter
½ cup celery	2 tablespoons flour
1 onion	

Wash and soak the dry split peas over night in the 2 quarts of cold water. Place in the soup kettle with the ham which has been skinned, the diced celery, sliced onion, and seasonings. Cover and simmer about 2 hours or bring to a boil and place in the oven at 275 degrees for 3 hours. Strain through a coarse strainer. Cream the butter and flour together. Add 1 cup of the warm soup stock slowly, stirring constantly. Then pour this slowly into the hot soup and stir until it reaches the boiling point to cook the flour.

Yield: 6 servings.

TOMATO SOUP

1 can tomatoes (1 quart)	3 allspice berries
1 cup water	12 peppercorns
1 cup fresh celery leaves	1 tablespoon salt
1 onion	4 tablespoons butter
4 whole cloves	¼ cup flour

Put all of the ingredients except the butter and flour in a pan. Cover and simmer for about 1 hour or cook in the oven at 275 degrees for 3 hours. Then strain.

Melt the butter and mix the flour with it. Then add a small portion of the strained tomato mixture. Stir and cook until it thickens. Continue adding the strained tomato in portions. Stir and cook after each addition. When the soup reaches the boiling point after the last portion of strained tomato has been added, it is ready to serve.

Yield: 6 servings.

TOMATO SOUP WITH MEAT STOCK

2½ to 3 pounds soup bone	1 cup carrots, cubed
2 tablespoons fat	2½ cups strained tomato
½ cup chopped onion	2 quarts cold water
1½ cups celery or celery	2 teaspoons salt
leaves	⅛ teaspoon pepper

Cut half the meat from the bone and cut it into cubes. Brown the cubes in the fat. Then brown the onion, celery and carrots slightly. Put the bone with the remaining meat and the rest of the ingredients in a kettle. Cover and simmer for about 2 hours or bring to a boil and place in the oven at 275 degrees for 3 hours. Strain. If it is too fat, cool it and skim the fat from it. Then reheat and serve.

Yield: 6 servings.

VEAL BROTH

1 knuckle of veal	1 onion
8 cups water	1 tablespoon salt
2 cups celery	⅛ teaspoon pepper
2 cups carrots	

Place the knuckle of veal, which has been cracked at the butcher's, in a large kettle and sear. While it is searing, prepare the vegetables. Wash and chop them fine. Add the cold water, vegetables and seasonings to the veal. Other vegetables may be used, but for Veal Broth, delicate flavors are desirable. Cover and simmer for about 2 hours or bring to a boil and place in the oven at 275 degrees for 3 hours.

Yield: 6 servings.

VEGETABLE SOUP WITHOUT STOCK

2 tablespoons butter	1 cup cabbage
1 onion	5 cups boiling water
1 cup carrots	½ cup tomato juice
1 cup potatoes	1 tablespoon salt
1 cup celery	¼ teaspoon pepper

Add the sliced onion to the butter and brown. Add the diced vegetables to the boiling water and strained tomato juice. Add the browned onions and other seasonings. Let simmer for about 1 hour or place in the oven at 275 degrees for 3 hours. Any desired combination of vegetables may be used, other than that given.

Yield: 6 servings.

CHAPTER XII

VEGETABLES

Vegetables should be, for the most part, as attractively prepared and served as possible. They may be prepared in the oven with the remainder of an oven meal (see page 148), as well as on a surface burner. Sometimes the color of oven-cooked vegetables is not as attractive as when surface cooked, but the advantages of oven meals may, under some circumstances, offset the slight disadvantage of the changed color. When whole meals are prepared in the oven at one time, watching is unnecessary and more hours may be spent away from the kitchen in recreation or other work which cannot be delegated to a Red Wheel. Oven meals are prepared at a high temperature for a relatively short period of time or at a low temperature (275 degrees) for a longer period of time (3 hours).

Waterless cooking of vegetables (so-called because only a few tablespoons of water are used for this method) may be used, but care must be exercised in the preparation. Unless the vegetables are young and succulent and a very tight-fitting cover is placed on the pan, the vegetables may stick or burn, but when done in the oven, this method requires no watching.

To prepare vegetables for cooking, wash them carefully. Discard all parts that are blemished or decayed. Then peel or scrape, as desired, or for some vegetables the skin may be left on.

Greens should be cooked in only the water that clings to the leaves after washing. Carrots, celery, tomatoes and summer squash require only a small amount of boiling salted water. This necessitates more or less constant watching. The remainder of the vegetables should be placed in sufficient boiling salted water to cover.

It is easy to spoil the flavor and appearance of vegetables by over-cooking. Even though they are valuable for the vitamins, mineral salts and to provide bulk, they will not be eaten if they look unappetizing and, therefore, will not provide these necessary qualities in the diet. Some vitamins and some mineral salts may be lost during cooking but tomato juice, or a few raw vegetables served as salads, will help to keep the supply adequate.

125

Most vegetables may be served with melted or Maître d'Hôtel butter or with a cream sauce. Some vegetables are especially good with Hollandaise or a Vinaigrette Sauce. When cold, many of them make pleasing salads, either alone or in combination, and with mayonnaise or French dressing.

Some vegetables are especially good after boiling when mashed or browned in the oven; over a surface burner, or broiled. There are many ways to prepare and serve the large varieties of vegetables, giving an opportunity for menus that are different.

ASPARAGUS

2 pounds asparagus   1 teaspoon salt
Boiling water

Wash and remove the tough ends from the asparagus. Add boiling water to cover and the salt. Boil for about 20 minutes, or until tender. If prepared in the oven, use only ½ cup boiling water and bake, covered, at 400 degrees for 40 minutes or at 275 degrees for 3 hours, substituting cold water if the latter temperature is used.

Yield: 6 servings.

BEANS (GREEN OR YELLOW)

1½ pounds beans   ¾ teaspoon salt
Boiling water

Clean and string the beans and break them into pieces. Add boiling water to cover and the salt. Boil for about 35 minutes, or until tender. If prepared in the oven, use only ¾ cup boiling water and bake, covered, at 400 degrees for 1 hour or at 275 degrees for 3 hours.

Yield: 6 servings.

BOSTON BAKED BEANS

Temperature, 300 degrees; Time, 6 hours

1 quart navy beans
¾ pound salt pork
1 tablespoon salt

3 tablespoons sugar
1 tablespoon molasses

Wash and soak the beans over night in cold water to cover. In the morning drain them and cover with fresh water. Cook over a surface burner until the skins burst, then drain. Scald the rind of the pork and scrape it well. Cut through the pork every ½ inch, making the cuts one inch deep. Put the beans in a pot and bury the pork in them. Mix the seasonings and molasses with 1 cup of boiling water and pour over the beans, then add enough more boiling water to cover them. As they become dry during the baking period add more water. Cover and bake at 300 degrees for 5½ hours. At the end of this time uncover them and bake them ½ hour longer to brown the top of the pork.

Yield: 8 servings.

BEETS

8 or 9 young beets   Boiling water

Wash medium-sized beets well. Leave at least an inch of the tops attached. Cover with the boiling water and cook until tender, or about 50 to 60 minutes for young beets. If prepared in the oven, use only 1 cup boiling water and bake, covered, at 400 degrees for 1½ hours or at 275 degrees for 3 hours. Old beets require considerably longer time for cooking than the young ones.

Yield: 6 servings.

BROCCOLI

1 bunch broccoli   1½ teaspoons salt
Boiling water

Wash the broccoli in salted water. Add the water to cover and the salt. Boil until tender, or about 45 minutes. If prepared in the oven, cover it and bake at 400 degrees for 1 hour or at 275 degrees for 3 hours, substituting cold water if the latter temperature is used.

Yield: 6 servings.

BRUSSELS SPROUTS

1 quart sprouts   1 teaspoon salt
Boiling water

Wash the sprouts carefully and remove all blemished leaves. Add the water to cover and the salt. Boil until tender, or about 15 minutes. If prepared in the oven, cover it and bake at 400 degrees for 40 to 45 minutes, or at 275 degrees for 3 hours, substituting cold water if the latter temperature is used.

Yield: 6 servings.

CABBAGE

3 pounds cabbage   1½ teaspoons salt
Boiling water

Wash and cut the cabbage into pieces and remove the heart. Add boiling water to cover and the salt. Boil until tender, or about 15 minutes. If prepared in the oven, cover it and bake at 400 degrees for 45 minutes or at 275 degrees for 3 hours, substituting cold water if the latter temperature is used.

Yield: 6 servings.

SCALLOPED CABBAGE

Temperature, 350 degrees; Time, 1 hour

4 cups cooked cabbage
4 tablespoons flour
2 teaspoons salt

⅛ teaspoon pepper
4 tablespoons butter
1½ cups milk

Put a layer of cabbage in a buttered baking dish. Add ⅛ of the flour, salt, pepper and butter. Continue in this manner until all of the ingredients are used. Add the milk. Bake uncovered at 350 degrees for 1 hour.

Yield: 6 servings.

CARROTS

2 pounds young carrots
Boiling water

1 teaspoon salt
3 tablespoons butter

Wash, scrape and cut the carrots in cubes or lengthwise strips. Add boiling water to barely cover and salt. Boil for about 25 minutes, or until tender. If prepared in the oven, use only ¼ cup boiling water and bake, covered, at 400 degrees for 1 hour or at 275 degrees for 3 hours. Add the butter and serve. After the carrots are buttered, they may be browned in the oven for 15 minutes at 400 degrees.

Yield: 6 servings.

BRAISED CARROTS

Temperature, 400 degrees; Time, 1 hour

2 pounds carrots
¼ cup butter

1 teaspoon salt

Cut the carrots into cubes or lengthwise strips. Place in a baking dish and add the butter and salt. Cover and bake at 400 degrees for 40 minutes, then uncover and bake for 20 minutes longer.

Yield: 6 servings.

CAULIFLOWER

1 large head cauliflower   2 teaspoons salt
Boiling water

Remove the stem and break the cauliflower into sections. Wash well. Add the boiling water to cover and the salt. Boil until tender, or about 30 minutes. If prepared in the oven, cover it and bake at 400 degrees for 45 minutes, or at 275 degrees for 3 hours, substituting cold water if the latter temperature is used.

Yield: 6 servings.

CELERY

4 bunches celery (3 stalks each)   1½ teaspoons salt
Boiling water

Wash and scrape the celery and cut into desired lengths. Add boiling water to barely cover and the salt. Boil about 25 minutes, or until tender. If prepared in the oven, use only 1 cup boiling water and bake, covered, at 400 degrees for 50 minutes or at 275 degrees for 3 hours.

Yield: 6 servings.

BRAISED CELERY

Temperature, 400 degrees; Time, 50 to 60 minutes

4 bunches celery (3 stalks   1 bouillon cube
  each)   3 tablespoons butter
1 cup boiling water   ½ teaspoon salt

Wash and scrape the celery. Cut in 2-inch lengths and put in a baking dish. Dissolve the bouillon cube in the water and add it, with the remaining ingredients, to the celery. Cover and bake at 400 degrees for 50 to 60 minutes.

Yield: 6 servings.

BAKED CORN PUDDING

Temperature, 400 degrees; Time, 40 minutes

2 cups corn	1 teaspoon salt
2 eggs	⅛ teaspoon pepper
1 cup milk	

Cut the corn from the cob and put in a buttered baking dish. Beat the eggs, add the milk and seasonings. Pour this mixture over the corn and bake in a pan set in boiling water at 400 degrees for 40 minutes.

Yield: 6 servings.

CORN SOUFFLÉ

Temperature, 325 degrees; Time, 1 hour

4 tablespoons butter	½ cup milk
5 tablespoons flour	3 egg yolks
½ teaspoon salt	1 cup canned corn
⅛ teaspoon pepper	3 egg whites

Melt the butter, add the flour and seasonings. Then add the scalded milk gradually, stirring constantly. Cool and add the beaten yolks, and then the corn. When it is in season, fresh corn may be used in place of canned. Fold in the beaten whites and bake at 325 degrees for 1 hour in a dish set in boiling water.

Yield: 6 servings.

OVEN STEWED CORN

Temperature, 400 degrees; Time, 50 minutes

4 cups corn	⅛ teaspoon pepper
1 cup milk	3 tablespoons butter
1 teaspoon salt	

Cut the corn from the cob and add the milk and seasonings. Place in a baking dish, cover, and bake at 400 degrees for 50 minutes. Remove from the oven and add the butter. For variation: 1 chopped green pepper may be added to the corn before baking.

Yield: 6 servings.

BAKED STUFFED EGG PLANT

Temperature, 375 degrees; Time, 30 to 35 minutes

1 egg plant	1 cup minced meat
1 tablespoon minced onion	½ cup bread crumbs
1 tablespoon butter	1 egg
3 tomatoes	1 teaspoon salt

Cut the egg plant from the shell. Cook the onion in the butter. Add it to the meat, egg plant and fresh tomatoes, which have been skinned and quartered. Either chicken, pork, or veal may be used. Cook for 15 minutes over a surface burner. Then add the egg and salt. Fill the shell with this mixture. Cover with buttered crumbs and bake at 375 degrees for 30 to 35 minutes.

Yield: 6 servings.

LIMA BEANS

1 quart fresh lima beans	1½ teaspoons salt
Boiling water	

Wash well and add the boiling water to cover and the salt. Boil for about 30 to 40 minutes, or until tender. If prepared in the oven, use only ½ cup of boiling water and bake, covered, at 400 degrees for 50 to 60 minutes or at 275 degrees for 3 hours.

Yield: 6 servings.

LIMA BEANS AND TOMATOES

Temperature, 275 degrees; Time, 3 hours

1⅛ cups dried lima beans	1¼ teaspoons salt
2 tablespoons fat	1 cup boiling water
1 green pepper	2 cups strained tomatoes
1½ tablespoons onion	

Soak the dried beans over night and in the morning drain them. Melt the fat and add the chopped pepper and onion. Brown over a surface burner. Add the remaining ingredients and heat. Pour into a buttered baking dish. Cover and bake at 275 degrees for 3 hours.

Yield: 6 servings.

CREAMED MUSHROOMS

1 pound mushrooms	2 tablespoons flour
1 pint milk	¼ teaspoon salt
3 tablespoons butter	⅟₁₆ teaspoon pepper

Heat the butter until it is slightly brown. Add the mushrooms that have been thoroughly washed and drained. Cook for about 3 or 4 minutes, stirring constantly. Add the flour and slowly add the milk and seasonings, stirring constantly until the mixture thickens. Place the saucepan over an asbestos mat, or place the mixture in a double boiler, and cook slowly for about 10 minutes. Serve over buttered rounds of toast.

Yield: 6 servings.

ONIONS

2 pounds onions	1½ teaspoons salt
Boiling water	

Peel small onions. Add the boiling water to cover and the salt. Boil for about 30 minutes, or until tender. If prepared in the oven, use only 1 cup of boiling water and bake, covered, at 400 degrees for 1¼ hours or at 275 degrees for 3 hours. The onions may then be buttered or creamed.

Yield: 6 servings.

PARSNIPS

2 pounds parsnips	1 teaspoon salt
Boiling water	

Peel and cut the parsnips in halves lengthwise. Add the boiling water to cover and the salt. Boil for about 35 minutes, or until tender. If prepared in the oven, use only ¾ cup of boiling water and bake, covered, at 400 degrees for 1 hour and 10 minutes or at 275 degrees for 3 hours.

Yield: 6 servings.

PEAS

4 pounds peas in pod   1 teaspoon salt
Boiling water

Shell the young peas and wash them. Add the water and salt. Boil for about 20 minutes, or until tender. If prepared in the oven, use only ¾ cup of boiling water and bake, covered, at 400 degrees for 35 to 40 minutes or at 275 degrees for 3 hours.

Yield: 6 servings.

BAKED POTATOES

Temperature, 450 degrees; Time, 50 to 60 minutes
or
Temperature, 275 degrees; Time, 3 hours*

Scrub 6 large potatoes, either sweet or white, and bake them at either of the above temperatures. If doing them at the lower temperature, place them in a covered casserole. The texture and flavor are somewhat different when the lower temperature is used.

Yield: 6 servings.

STUFFED BAKED POTATOES

Temperature, 450 degrees; Time, 50 to 60 minutes
then
Temperature, 475 degrees; Time, 12 minutes

6 potatoes   2 teaspoons salt
½ cup milk   ⅛ teaspoon pepper
3 tablespoons butter

Bake medium-sized potatoes at 450 degrees for 50 to 60 minutes. Cut in halves and remove the edible portion, taking care not to break the shell or skin. Mash them and add the milk, butter and seasonings. Beat the mixture until it is as light as mashed potatoes. Then return it to the potato shells. Put a bit of butter and a dash of paprika on each portion of potato. Place

* This time and temperature is suitable for oven meals.

the stuffed potatoes in a pan and bake, uncovered, at 475 degrees for 12 minutes, or until the filling is browned.

Yield: 6 servings.

BROWNED POTATOES

Temperature, 425 degrees; Time, 1 hour

2½ pounds potatoes
2 tablespoons flour

1½ teaspoons salt
4 tablespoons butter

Cut the potatoes into cubes or balls. Place in a shallow baking dish and add the flour, salt and butter. Bake, uncovered, at 425 degrees for 1 hour. When the potatoes have been in the oven for ½ hour, stir them.

Yield: 6 servings.

MASHED POTATOES

3 pounds potatoes
1½ teaspoons salt

¾ cup hot milk
4 tablespoons butter

Wash and peel the potatoes. Add the salt and enough boiling water to cover. Cover and boil for about 30 minutes, or until tender. Drain and mash. Add the milk and the melted butter, and beat thoroughly.

Yield: 6 servings.

MASHED POTATO PUFF

Temperature, 400 degrees; Time, 45 minutes

⅓ cup hot milk
2 tablespoons butter
½ teaspoon salt

⅛ teaspoon pepper
3 cups mashed potatoes
2 egg whites

Add the hot milk, butter and seasonings to the mashed potatoes (left-over potatoes may be used) and beat until smooth. Fold in the beaten egg whites and put into a greased baking dish. Bake at 400 degrees for 45 minutes.

Yield: 6 servings.

PARSLEY POTATOES

3 pounds potatoes
1½ teaspoons salt
Boiling water

2 tablespoons parsley
4 tablespoons butter

Wash and peel the potatoes. Cut them into balls or cubes.
Cover with boiling water and add the salt. Cook until tender,
or about 30 minutes. If prepared in the oven, add only ¼ cup
of boiling water to the potatoes and bake, covered, at either
400 degrees for 1 hour or 275 degrees for 3 hours. Then chop
the parsley fine, add it to the melted butter, and pour it over
the potatoes.

Yield: 6 servings.

SCALLOPED POTATOES

Temperature, 400 degrees; Time, 50 to 60 minutes
or
Temperature, 275 degrees; Time, 3 hours*

5 cups sliced potatoes
4 tablespoons butter
4 tablespoons flour

2 teaspoons salt
1½ cups milk

Wash, pare and slice the potatoes thin. In a buttered baking
dish put about ⅓ of the potatoes, butter, flour and salt. Prepare
other layers in this manner until all of the ingredients are used.
Add the milk and bake, uncovered, at either of the above temperatures.

Yield: 6 servings.

---

* This time and temperature is suitable for oven meals.

BOILED SWEET POTATOES

3 medium-sized potatoes   Boiling water

Scrub the potatoes and to them add boiling water to cover. Cover and boil until tender, or about 50 minutes. Then drain and peel.

These may be served plain with butter. For a pleasing variation, mash the potatoes and to them add 2 teaspoons of salt and sufficient hot milk to moisten if they are dry. Form into patties and roll them in 1½ cups of crushed corn flakes. Put the patties into a well-buttered pan and dot them with butter. Bake at 400 degrees for 20 minutes.

Yield: 6 servings.

CANDIED SWEET POTATOES

Temperature, 400 degrees; Time, 1 hour

6 potatoes   ¼ cup water
½ cup brown sugar   3 tablespoons butter

Pare the potatoes and cut lengthwise into halves. Put in a shallow baking dish. Cover and bake at 400 degrees for 30 minutes. Then make a syrup by boiling the sugar and water together for 3 minutes. Add the butter and add this syrup to the potatoes. Bake, uncovered, at 400 degrees for 30 minutes longer.

If previously cooked potatoes are used, add the syrup and bake for 35 minutes at 400 degrees.

Yield: 6 servings.

CASSEROLE OF SWEET POTATOES

Temperature, 400 degrees; Time, 1 hour
or
Temperature, 275 degrees; Time, 3 hours*

3 pounds sweet potatoes 1 teaspoon salt
3 tablespoons butter

Pare and cut sweet potatoes in halves lengthwise or smaller pieces if the potatoes are very large. Place in a casserole with the butter and salt. Cover and bake at 400 degrees for 1 hour or at 275 degrees for 3 hours. If previously cooked potatoes are used, they may be baked at 400 degrees for 35 minutes.

If the potatoes are an extremely dry variety, add from $\frac{1}{4}$ to $\frac{1}{2}$ cup of water to prevent them from drying out during the baking period.

Yield: 6 servings.

BOILED RICE

1 cup rice 2 teaspoons salt
2 quarts boiling water

Either polished or brown rice may be used. Wash the rice. Add it slowly to the boiling salted water. Boil rapidly until the rice is tender, or about $\frac{1}{2}$ hour, or place in cold salted water in a covered dish and bake at 275 degrees for 3 hours. Drain and rinse with either hot or cold water. The cold water will serve to separate the grains better, making each one distinct. If this is desired and the cold water is used, the rice will have to be reheated before serving. This can be done by placing it in the oven for a few minutes.

Yield: 6 servings.

---

* This time and temperature is suitable for oven meals.

SPINACH

3 pounds spinach   2½ teaspoons salt

Remove the roots and thick stems from the spinach and wash it carefully in several waters. Put in a large pan and add the salt. Simmer gently until tender—about 10 minutes—or cover and bake at 400 degrees for 20 to 25 minutes; or at 350 degrees for 30 to 35 minutes. Serve with melted butter and a slice of lemon.

Yield: 6 servings.

SQUASH

Temperature, 400 degrees; Time, 1½ hours
or
Temperature, 450 degrees; Time 30 minutes
then
*Temperature, 275 degrees; Time, 3 hours**

½ large dry winter squash   1½ teaspoons salt
2 tablespoons butter

Remove the seeds and strings. The squash may be left in quarters or halves, as desired, and baked in the shell. Place in a pan without any water and cover. Bake at either of the above temperatures. After the squash is tender, it can be removed from the shell by scraping. Mash and add the butter and salt. Beat well together. If desired, it can be served in the shell, seasoned, and melted butter added to it. It can also be removed from the shell, seasoned and melted butter poured over without mashing.

Yield: 6 servings.

---

*This time and temperature is suitable for oven meals.

BAKED STUFFED TOMATOES

Temperature, 450 degrees; Time, 15 to 20 minutes

6 tomatoes	½ teaspoon salt
2 cups bread cubes	½ teaspoon paprika
12 stuffed olives, chopped	2 tablespoons butter
2 tablespoons parsley, chopped	

Wash very firm tomatoes and make a cavity in each. Mix the bread, olives and seasonings together to make a filling. Fill each cavity and put about ½ teaspoon of butter on top of each tomato. Bake at 450 degrees for 15 to 20 minutes.

Yield: 6 servings.

STEWED TOMATOES AND ONIONS

3 cups tomatoes (canned or fresh)	2 teaspoons salt
	⅛ teaspoon pepper
1 cup sliced onions	1 tablespoon butter

Put all of the ingredients in a baking dish and stir to mix well. If fresh tomatoes are used, remove the stems and skins and cut the tomatoes into eighths. Cover and bake at 400 degrees for 50 minutes or at 275 degrees for 3 hours; or simmer slowly on the surface burner for about 20 minutes.

Yield: 6 servings.

SCALLOPED TOMATOES AND CHEESE

Temperature, 400 degrees; Time, ½ hour

8 tomatoes	2 tablespoons butter
1½ teaspoons salt	2 cups stale bread cubes
⅛ teaspoon pepper	⅓ cup cheese

Scald the tomatoes to remove the skins. Cut the tomatoes into pieces and place in a baking dish. Add the salt and pepper and cover with the bread cubes mixed with 2 tablespoons of melted butter. Sprinkle with the ⅓ cup of grated cheese and bake at 400 degrees for ½ hour.

Yield: 6 servings.

TURNIPS

2 pounds turnips   1½ teaspoons salt
Boiling water

Peel and cut the turnips into halves or cubes. Cover with boiling salted water and boil until tender, or about 20 to 30 minutes, or bake, covered, in the oven at 400 degrees for 1½ hours; or 275 degrees for 3 hours, substituting cold water if the latter temperature is used. Serve with melted butter.

Yield: 6 servings.

VEGETABLE CHOP SUEY

Temperature, 500 degrees for browning; Time, 15 minutes
then
Temperature, 275 degrees; Time, 3 hours

2 tablespoons butter   ⅓ cup rice
½ cup onions   1 bouillon cube
1½ cups celery   1½ teaspoons salt
1 green pepper   ⅛ teaspoon pepper
1 cup mushrooms, sliced   3½ cups cold water

Put the butter in a casserole and, when melted, add the sliced onions. Brown over a surface burner or in the oven at 500 degrees while preparing the rest of the vegetables. When the onions are brown, add the remaining sliced vegetables, rice, bouillon cube, seasonings and water. Cover and bake at 275 degrees for 3 hours.

Yield: 6 servings.

CHAPTER XIII

MISCELLANEOUS

SALTED ALMONDS

Temperature, 350 degrees; Time, 30 minutes

1 pound almond meats   1 tablespoon salt
2½ tablespoons olive oil

Pour boiling water over the almonds and when cool remove the skins. Place them in a shallow pan and add the remaining ingredients. Mix and put in the oven at 350 degrees for 30 minutes. Stir twice during the baking time.

APPLE SAUCE

Temperature, 400 degrees; Time, 30 to 35 minutes
or
Temperature, 275 degrees; Time, 1½ hours

4 pounds tart apples   4 tablespoons butter
1½ cups sugar   1½ cups cold water
2 teaspoons cinnamon

Peel, core and cut the apples into quarters. Wash them well and place in a casserole. Sprinkle with the sugar and cinnamon and dot with butter. Add the water, cover and bake at 400 degrees for 30 to 35 minutes, or at 275 degrees for 1½ hours. Remove from the oven and stir well.

Yield: 8 servings.

STEWED APRICOTS

Temperature, 400 degrees; Time, 1 hour
or
Temperature, 275 degrees; Time, 3 hours*

1 pound apricots   3 cups water
¾ cup sugar

Wash the apricots well. Soak over night in clean water to cover (about 3 cups). Add the sugar in the morning. Place in the oven at 400 degrees for 1 hour. If they are to be stewed at the whole meal temperature for 3 hours, soaking is unnecessary.

Yield: 6 servings.

---

* This time and temperature is suitable for oven meals.

DRIP COFFEE

Use pulverized coffee and measure 1 level tablespoon for each cup. Place in perforated cylinder. Measure fresh boiling water, allowing ¾ of a measuring cup for each cup of coffee desired. Pour over the coffee. Be sure the coffee pot is heated before using and that it is kept hot during the time the water is dripping through the grounds. If stronger coffee is desired either more coffee may be allowed for each cup or the water may be poured over the coffee a second time.

PERCOLATED COFFEE

Use finely ground coffee. Allow 1 level tablespoon for each cup. Place in the percolator. Allow ¾ of a measuring cup of fresh water for each cup. Add the water and percolate for 12 to 15 minutes after circulation starts in the pot.

BOILED COFFEE

Use coarsely ground coffee. Measure 2 level tablespoons for each cup. Add a clean crushed egg shell and enough cold water to moisten the grounds. Add ¾ of a measuring cup of freshly boiled water for each cup to be made. Bring to the boiling point. Remove from the fire but keep hot for 5 minutes to allow the grounds to settle. Strain and serve.

BAKED CORN OMELET

Temperature, 325 degrees; Time, 25 minutes

1 tablespoon butter	1 tablespoon flour
2 cups fresh corn	¾ teaspoon salt
4 eggs	⅛ teaspoon pepper

Heat the butter in a frying pan over a surface burner. Put the corn in a sauce pan and heat. Separate the eggs and beat the whites and then the yolks. Add the flour, heated corn and seasoning to the yolks. Fold in the beaten egg whites. Pour into the hot frying pan and bake at 325 degrees for 25 minutes.

Yield: 6 servings.

143

CRANBERRY JELLY

Temperature, 450 degrees; Time, 25 minutes

1 quart cranberries   2 cups sugar
1 cup water

Wash the cranberries and put them with the water in a baking dish. Cover and bake at 450 degrees for 20 minutes. Add the sugar, stirring well. Return to the oven and cook 5 minutes longer. Then strain them if desired. If the jelly is to be served with a roast it may be made while the meat is searing at 450 degrees.

BAKED EGGS

Temperature, 275 degrees; Time, 12 to 15 minutes

Break as many eggs as desired into individual ramekins or custard cups which have been well buttered. Bake uncovered at 275 degrees for 12 to 15 minutes. They can be seasoned to taste just before serving with salt and pepper and additional butter if desired. If 5 or 6 eggs are baked together in a large baking dish bake them at 275 degrees for ½ hour.

EGGS POACHED IN MILK

Temperature, 350 degrees; Time, 15 to 17 minutes

6 eggs   ½ teaspoon salt
1/16 teaspoon pepper   6 tablespoons milk or cream

Butter 6 individual ramekins well. Break an egg into each. Sprinkle with salt and pepper and add 1 tablespoon of milk or cream to each one. Place in a shallow pan containing boiling water. Cover the pan and bake at 350 degrees for 15 to 17 minutes.

Yield: 6 servings.

MALT BREAKFAST FOOD

Temperature, 400 degrees; Time, 35 minutes

4 cups boiling water   1 teaspoon salt
                                 1 cup malt breakfast food

Put the salt and boiling water in the top of a double boiler. Gradually add the malt, stirring constantly. When all has been added cover and place over the lower part of a double boiler which has been filled to one-third of its capacity with boiling water. Put in the oven at 400 degrees for 35 minutes.

Yield: 6 servings.

OATMEAL

Temperature, 400 degrees; Time, 35 minutes

2 cups rolled oats   1 teaspoon salt
4 cups boiling water

Add the oatmeal to the boiling salted water in the top of a double boiler. Put this in the lower part of the double boiler which has been filled to one-third of its capacity with boiling water. Put in the oven and cook at 400 degrees for 35 minutes.

Yield: 6 servings.

LORAIN OVEN OMELET

Temperature, 325 degrees; Time, 20 minutes

4 eggs   ½ teaspoon salt
4 tablespoons milk   1 tablespoon butter

Beat the egg yolks and add the 4 tablespoons of milk which have been heated. Add the salt and then carefully fold in the egg whites which have been beaten until they are stiff. Heat the butter in a frying pan on a surface burner and pour the omelet in it. Place in the oven at 325 degrees for 20 minutes. If a larger omelet is desired do not increase the number of eggs, but make two omelets.

Yield: 5 servings.

OVEN CODDLED EGGS

Temperature, 275 degrees; Time, 18 to 20 minutes

Place the eggs in the unbroken shells in a heavy baking dish with no water in it. Bake at 275 degrees for 18 to 20 minutes. When they are done they may be served in any way that a soft cooked egg would be served.

STEWED PEACHES

Temperature, 400 degrees; Time, 1 hour
or
Temperature, 275 degrees; Time, 3 hours*

Use the same method as for Stewed Apricots (see p. 142).

Yield: 6 to 8 servings.

SALTED PEANUTS

Temperature, 350 degrees; Time, 1 hour

1½ pounds peanut meats   1 tablespoon salt
2½ tablespoons olive oil

Put the peanuts in boiling water and when cool remove the skins. Place them in a shallow pan with the remaining ingredients. Put in the oven at 350 degrees for 1 hour, stirring every 15 minutes.

STEWED PRUNES

Temperature, 400 degrees; Time, 1 hour
or
Temperature, 275 degrees; Time, 3 hours*

1 pound prunes   3 cups water
½ cup sugar   2 tablespoons lemon juice

Use the same method as for Stewed Apricots (see p. 142). Add the lemon juice after the prunes have been removed from the oven, or cook with several slices of lemon in it.

Yield: 6 to 8 servings.

---

* This time and temperature is suitable for oven meals.

STEWED PRUNES WITH CRANBERRY SAUCE

Temperature, 400 degrees; Time, 1½ hours

1 pound prunes
4 cups water

1 pound cranberries
1½ cups sugar

Wash the prunes and soak them in the 4 cups of water over night. The next day cover them and place in the oven at 400 degrees for 1 hour. Remove from the oven and drain the juice from them. Add enough water to the juice to make 2 cups of liquid. Add the cranberries and sugar to this. Stir to dissolve the sugar. Cover and place in the oven at 400 degrees for 30 minutes. Remove the pits from the prunes and place in a serving dish. Pour this Cranberry Sauce over them.

Yield: 8 servings.

OVEN COOKED RHUBARB

Temperature, 400 degrees; Time, 25 to 30 minutes

6 cups rhubarb

⅔ cup sugar

Wash and cut the rhubarb into pieces. Early rhubarb does not need to be skinned. Later the skin becomes tough and should be removed. Place in a baking dish. Add the sugar and bake at 400 degrees for 25 to 30 minutes.

Yield: 4 or 5 servings.

MELBA TOAST

Temperature, 325 degrees; Time, 15 to 18 minutes

Slice day old bread very thin. Put slices on a pan side by side and place in the oven at 325 degrees for 15 to 18 minutes.

CHAPTER XIV

WHOLE MEAL COOKERY

Oven meals are so called because the whole dinner may be prepared in the oven at one time. This development has been brought about by means of the Lorain Oven Heat Regulator.

It is a great saving of time to be able to place a whole meal in the oven, adjust the Red Wheel to the desired temperature, and then go away and forget the meal until the end of the time for properly cooking it.

Some meals can be prepared at high temperatures for short periods of time, and some at low temperatures for comparatively long periods of time.

The choice of high or low temperatures will depend on how long it is desirable to be away from the kitchen. By using a low temperature it is possible to forget the meal for several hours after it is in the oven and the Red Wheel adjusted. This allows time for shopping, recreation, or other work which needs consecutive time for accomplishing. A temperature of 275 degrees is generally accepted as suitable for a 3-hour meal.

If whole meals are to be prepared in the oven at one time select foods which should be baked at the same temperature and, as far as possible, for the same length of time.

The menus given in this book are suggestive of combinations of foods which can be selected and prepared in the oven at the same time. If the recipes require different lengths of time, those requiring the longest time should be started first and the rest put in the oven later. Plan to have everything in long enough before the meal is to be served so all will be done at the same time.

See the Index for the recipes given in these menus.

Breakfasts

Temperature, 400 degrees; Time, 35 minutes

Baked Apples

Oatmeal   Cream

Bacon   Muffins

Coffee

———

Temperature, 400 degrees; Time, 35 minutes

Fresh Fruit

Baked Liver   Corn Bread

Coffee

———

Temperature, 400 degrees; Time, 30 to 35 minutes

Apple Sauce

Baked Sausage   Coffee Cake

Coffee

———

Temperature, 400 degrees; Time, 35 minutes

Oven Cooked Rhubarb

Malt Breakfast Food

Muffins   Marmalade

Coffee

Temperature, 450 degrees; Time, 30 minutes
then
Temperature, 350 degrees; Time, 15 minutes

Canned Fruit
Eggs Poached in Milk   Popovers
Coffee

———

Temperature, 325 degrees; Time, 20 minutes

Orange Juice
Ready-to-Eat Cereal
Lorain Oven Omelet   Melba Toast
Coffee

•   •   •   •

Luncheons

Temperature, 400 degrees; Time, 1 hour

Sweetbread Timbales
Parsley Potatoes   Salad
Tea   Cookies

———

Temperature, 400 degrees; Time, 1 hour

Veal and Noodles
Stewed Tomatoes and Onions
Fresh Fruit

150

Temperature, 350 degrees; Time, 50 minutes

Macaroni and Cheese   Spinach
Crisp Pickles
Grapefruit

———

Temperature, 425 degrees; Time, 1 hour

Baked Lamb Croquettes
Browned Potatoes   Muffins
Fruit Tarts

———

Temperature, 400 degrees; Time, 1 hour

Scalloped Potatoes and Ham
Pepper Relish   Corn Muffins
Lorain Canned Fruit

❋   ❋   ❋   ❋

Note: When pies or shortcakes are being done the meat can be seared at a little lower temperature for a longer time.

Dinners

Temperature, 500 degrees for searing; Time, 15 minutes
then
Temperature, 400 degrees; Time, 1 hour

Baked Veal Cutlets   Scalloped Potatoes
Yellow Beans
Individual Chocolate Puddings   Custard Sauce

Temperature, 400 degrees; Time, 1 hour

Beef Loaf   Tomato Sauce
      Braised Celery
          Salad
Baked Apples   Cookies
    Cheese   Crackers
          Coffee

———

Temperature, 400 degrees; Time, 45 minutes

*Chicken or Turkey Loaf
Mushroom Sauce   Mashed Potato Puff
          Salad
      Peach Roly Poly

———

Temperature, 350 degrees; Time, 1 hour

*Veal and Rice Ring   Scalloped Cabbage
          Salad
Gingerbread Custard   Foamy Sauce

———

Temperature, 275 degrees; Time, 3 hours

Maryland Chicken   Currant Jelly
    Boiled Rice   Peas
    Sponge Cake   Butterscotch Sauce

---

* These recipes are suggestive of ways to use left overs.

Temperature, 500 degrees for searing; Time, 20 to 30 minutes
then
Temperature, 275 degrees; Time, 3 hours

Bouillon   Toast Triangles
Roast Goose or Turkey
Apple Sauce   Spiced Peaches
Casserole of Sweet Potatoes
Buttered Turnips
Celery
Steamed Plum Pudding   Currant Hard Sauce
Coffee

———

Temperature, 500 degrees for searing; Time, 15 to 20 minutes
then
Temperature, 275 degrees; Time, 3 hours

Boned Smoked Shoulder of Pork   Horseradish Sauce
Baked Potatoes (en casserole)
Onions
Salad   French Dressing
Apricot and Rice Pudding   Apricot Sauce

———

Temperature, 450 degrees for searing; Time, 20 to 30 minutes
then
Temperature, 275 degrees; Time, 3 hours

Leg of Lamb   Parsley Potatoes
Baked Squash
Butterscotch Rolls*   Relish
Salad
Apricot Tarts†

———

* The rolls and tarts may be baked while the meat is searing.
† Prunes may be substituted for apricots.

153

Temperature, 500 degrees for searing; Time, 20 to 30 minutes
then
Temperature, 275 degrees; Time, 3 hours

Roast Pork   Casserole Sweet Potatoes
Apple Salad   French Dressing
Baked Turnips
Indian Pudding

———

Temperature, 450 degrees; Time, 1 hour

Baked Shad   Baked Potatoes
Baked Stuffed Tomatoes
Cucumber Salad
Peach Cobbler
Coffee

———

Temperature, 275 degrees; Time, 3 hours

Tomato Soup
Veal Birds   Boiled Rice
Asparagus
Cherry and Nut Salad   French Dressing
Date Pudding   Hard Sauce

CHAPTER XV

BROILING

Broiling is a quick method of cooking. It is accomplished by subjecting food to the direct heat of a fire. It helps to bring out the best flavor and makes the food extremely palatable and appetizing. The foods which are most often prepared in the broiler are meats, fish, poultry, toast, toasted sandwiches, vegetables, and sometimes whole meals. Broil only the choicest and most tender cuts of meat and young poultry. It is not worth while to try to broil the tougher varieties, as this method of cookery does not increase tenderness.

Broiling is an art. No absolutely definite directions can be given for accomplishing it because there are so many variations in the food which is to be prepared. Meat varies in quality, distribution of fat, thickness of the cut and the amount of bone. People vary in their standards of what constitutes rare, medium and well-done food. What is rare to one may seem medium well done to another. It is really necessary to learn by experience from the conditions in each home just how to master this art of broiling.

General Directions

Broil with the broiler door open. It is easier to watch the food as it broils. Any smoke which may form from the fat on the meat itself is not so noticeable in the room, as the open door helps to create a draft and the smoke is drawn up the flue. If flue connected, no odor of broiling meat will be noticeable in the room and, if not flue connected the odor will be less conspicuous.

Heat the broiler compartment for 10 or 12 minutes previous to the time the broiling operation is to start. If it is desirable

155

to sear the meat on both sides, the broiler pan may be preheated while the compartment is being heated. Otherwise remove the broiler pan and close the door during the preheating period if it is desirable to have the pan cold. The food may be placed on the unheated pan and then put into the previously heated broiler compartment. Place all food on the top section of the broiler pan.

After the broiler compartment has been preheated, place the broiler pan in a groove which will bring the food near enough to the flame so that it will brown the outer surface quickly. This distance will have to be judged by the thickness of the food, the size of the gas flame and the rapidity with which it is desirable to brown the product.

Meat must be turned in order to brown it on both sides and to cook it equally. If it is necessary to cook the food longer than merely to brown it, the gas flame may be decreased or the broiler pan moved farther from the flame to allow the heat to penetrate slowly to the interior, meanwhile cooking the food.

Meat tongs may be secured to turn the meat without penetrating it with a fork. If a fork is used, it should be inserted in the fat rather than in the fiber of the meat, as much juice may be lost when the fiber is pricked.

If it is desirable that the meat be basted, pull the broiler pan part way out from the compartment. Dip a spoon into the fat in the lower pan and pour the fat over the meat. This fat may help to brown the surface of the meat and the flavor is liked by many people.

For broiling meat rub a bit of the suet over the top section to grease it slightly. For broiling vegetables grease the pan with a bit of butter. If meats or fish do not contain a large amount of fat it may be necessary to add some before broiling. Some meats, such as bacon, pork and lamb chops, will have sufficient fat on them to grease the pan without the use of additional fat. Previously cooked vegetables may be browned on one side only but must be heated through if they are to be appetizing.

Appetizers

CANAPÉS

Cut rounds of bread from thin slices. Place on the top of the unheated broiler pan. Insert in broiler compartment about 3 inches from the flame. Toast on one side and spread the toasted side with melted butter. Combine one hard-cooked egg, which has been chopped very fine, with 3 tablespoons of pepper relish and 1 tablespoon of chili sauce. Spread this mixture on the rounds of bread and serve at the beginning of the meal as an appetizer.

*   *   *   *

Spread anchovy paste on rounds of bread which have been toasted on one side. Decorate with bits of chopped pickle and slices of crisp fresh radishes. Sprinkle with a few drops of onion juice. Caviar may be substituted for the anchovy paste, if desired.

*   *   *   *

Toast fingers may be made instead of toast rounds, and various combinations of appetizing morsels put on these little lengths of bread. They may be spread with butter, previously creamed with half as much prepared mustard and a dash of Worcestershire or Tabasco Sauce. Bits of left-over pickle or olive mixed with a little mayonnaise or canned salmon, onion, tomato, or any left-over relishes, provided the flavors blend well with one another, may be used for these appetizers.

Fish

FILLET OF HADDOCK

Place the haddock, from which the bones have been removed, in the well-oiled heated broiler pan with the top part removed. Put a small amount of oil over the top of the fish and place the pan in the heated broiler compartment. Broil for 15 to 18 minutes without turning. Sprinkle with salt and pepper and serve with Tartare Sauce.

HALIBUT

Select halibut steaks from ¾ to 1 inch thick. Wipe them clean and place them on the greased broiler pan without the top section. Place some melted butter or oil on the top of them. Put the pan in the heated broiler compartment and broil for about 25 minutes, turning when the steak is about half done. Sprinkle with salt and pepper and serve with melted butter and chopped parsley. Garnish with lemon cut in eighths from which the seeds have been removed. Cod steaks may be substituted for halibut, if desired.

LOBSTER

Purchase a live lobster and have it prepared for broiling. This preparation is accomplished by inserting a sharp knife carefully at the point where the tail and body shell come together, cutting the spinal cord. Split down the center and remove the stomach and intestinal vein. Broil as soon as possible after this is done. Preheat the broiler for 10 minutes. Place the lobster, meat side up, in the broiler pan without the top section and put in the heated broiling compartment. Broil for 7 minutes on the flesh side and 5 minutes on the shell side. Turn again and baste the flesh with melted butter. Broil 3 minutes longer. Crack the claws with a mallet. Serve with lemon and melted butter.

PLANKED FISH

Specially made planks can be purchased for cooking. Heat one of them slowly either in the oven or broiler. Then rub it with oil. For broiling clean the fish thoroughly. Split it down the back and remove the bones. Place the fish with the skin side down on the well-oiled and heated plank. Shad and White Fish are especially fine when prepared in this way. If other fish are used and are less fat, rub them with oil and then put into the heated broiler compartment so the fish will be about 2 inches from the flame. Let broil for about 30 minutes or until the fish is cooked. Remove from the broiler and season with salt and pepper. Have Duchess Potatoes (see p. 168) ready. Put them through a pastry bag and tube to form a border around the edge of the plank. Between the potatoes and fish any previously cooked hot vegetables may be placed, such as string beans, stuffed tomatoes or carrots. Brush the top of the potatoes with white of egg and then return to the broiler compartment with the flame turned low. Let it remain there until the potatoes have browned. Then remove it again from the broiler, garnish with lemon and parsley or watercress, and serve.

YELLOW PIKE

After the pike have been thoroughly cleaned, open them flat and place them, skin side down, on the well-greased broiler pan, without the top section, that has been heated in the broiler compartment for about 5 minutes. Brush the tops of the fish with melted butter or oil. Place on a rack in the heated broiler compartment so that the fish are about 2 inches from the flame. Broil until they are a delicate brown. This will take about 15 minutes. When they are removed from the broiler, season with salt and pepper and a little more melted butter. Sprinkle with chopped parsley and serve with thin slices of lemon.

SALMON

Put the salmon steaks, which have been carefully wiped, in the greased broiler pan, without the top section. Place it in the heated broiler compartment and broil for about 25 minutes, turning when the salmon is about half done. Sprinkle with salt and pepper. Serve on a platter or chop plate garnished with parsley, slices of sour pickles and lemon.

WHITE FISH

Remove the bones from the fish and open it out flat. Place the broiler pan in the broiler compartment while it is being pre-heated. Grease the broiler pan well and put the fish, skin side down, on it without the top section. Brush with melted butter or brush with oil. Place in the heated broiler compartment and broil for 15 minutes, or until it is brown. Then reduce the heat, or lower the broiler pan away from the flame, and broil slowly for 10 minutes longer. When it is removed from the broiler, season with salt and pepper and a little more melted butter. Sprinkle with chopped parsley and serve with thin slices of lemon.

Meats

BACON

Select evenly sliced bacon with well-distributed fat and lean and no gristle. Place strips on the top section in the broiler pan and put the pan in the heated broiler compartment. Broil for about 3 minutes, turning to brown the other side at the end of half the time. The length of time depends on the thickness and the quality of the bacon. Remove to a platter and garnish with parsley. Broiled bacon may be used as a garnish for poached eggs, vegetable dishes of many kinds, or with meats and fish.

FILLET MIGNON

Brush the fillets with melted butter and place on the well-greased top section of the broiler pan. Put the pan in the heated broiler compartment. Sear the steaks for 3 minutes. Turn and sear on the other side for 2 or 3 minutes longer. Season with salt and pepper. Add ¼ teaspoon of butter to each fillet and serve.

HAM

Select a slice of ham about ¼ inch thick for broiling. Cut through the edges in several places to prevent the meat from curling. Place on the top section in the broiler pan and put the pan in the heated broiler compartment. Broil for 18 to 20 minutes, turning frequently to prevent the fat from charring and to insure uniform cooking. Serve garnished with crisp watercress.

HAMBURG CAKES

| 1 pound ground round steak | ⅛ teaspoon pepper |
| 2 teaspoons salt | ½ onion, chopped fine |

Mix the seasonings with the ground meat and onion. Press into small flat cakes. Put on the top section in the broiler pan and place in the heated broiler compartment. Sear one side, then turn the cakes and sear the other side. Broil about 15 minutes, turning the cakes from one side to the other so they will be evenly cooked. Remove to a platter and serve with a Parsley Butter Sauce.

HAMBURG STEAK

1 pound ground round steak
1½ teaspoons salt
⅛ teaspoon pepper

½ small onion, grated
2 tablespoons green
   pepper, chopped

Put all of the ingredients in a mixing bowl. Mix well and pat into oblong shape until ½ inch thick. Place on the buttered top section and put in the heated broiler compartment. Broil for 7 minutes, then turn and broil 7 minutes longer.

This steak may be done with vegetables prepared for broiling surrounding it. It makes a very attractive, easily and quickly prepared meal, especially when served with suitable garnishes.

HASH

3 cups left-over meat
3 cups potatoes
1 onion
⅔ cup left-over gravy

1½ teaspoons salt
¼ teaspoon pepper
3 tablespoons butter

Mix the chopped left-over meat and chopped boiled potatoes with the rest of the ingredients except the butter. Put in a well-greased shallow baking dish. Put bits of the butter over the top. Place in the heated broiler compartment so that the top of the dish is about 3 inches from the flame. When the hash is brown on top (after about 10 minutes), turn the flame down to half and leave it in 15 minutes longer.

LAMB CHOPS

Lamb chops for broiling should be about 1½ inches thick. Either loin or rib chops may be selected. Place on the top section in the broiler pan and put the pan in the heated broiler compartment. Sear well on both sides. Turn the flame low and broil for 12 to 15 minutes, turning the chops when they are about half done so as to let the heat penetrate evenly from both sides. Season with salt, pepper and butter.

CALF'S LIVER AND BACON

Have the liver sliced about ½ inch thick. Remove the veins and skin. Wipe well. Put on the greased top section in the broiler pan and place in the heated broiler compartment. Turn after the one side has seared. Put strips of bacon over the top and turn them when the upper side has become brown. Remove the bacon as soon as it is brown and continue broiling the liver. Calf's liver will broil in 10 minutes, but it must be turned frequently while broiling so it will be evenly cooked.

PORK CHOPS

Broil pork chops from ¾ to 1 inch thick. Place on the top section in the broiler pan in the heated broiler compartment. Sear on both sides for 5 minutes, then turn the flame low and broil for 10 minutes longer, turning the chops again to let the heat penetrate evenly from both sides.

SAUSAGE CAKES

Press sausage cakes about ½ inch thick. Place on the top section in the broiler pan and put it in the heated broiler compartment. Broil for 8 or 9 minutes, turning the cakes when brown on one side.

LINK SAUSAGE

Put small sausage links on the top section in the broiler pan and place in the heated broiler compartment. Broil for 4 minutes, then turn the links and broil about 3½ minutes longer.

PLANKED STEAK

Place a choice porterhouse steak, cut about 2 inches thick, on a special and seasoned plank. Put salt around the steak on the plank about ¼ to ½ inch thick. This protects the plank from burning while the steak is being broiled. Insert it into the heated broiler compartment so that the meat is about 1½ inches from the flame. Sear the meat on one side, then turn and sear on the other. Either move the plank to a lower rack or turn the flame lower and broil the steak according to the directions given for Porterhouse Steak. Remove from the broiler, scrape the salt from the plank and wipe carefully to remove it all. Prepare a border of potatoes by using the recipe for Duchess Potatoes (see p. 168), and putting them through a pastry bag and tube in rosette or fancy shapes around the edge of the plank. Fill the space between the potatoes and the steak with any vegetables that have been previously cooked. Season the steak with salt and pepper and brush the top of the potatoes with egg whites. Return to the broiler to brown the potatoes and serve garnished with thin slices of tomato and cucumber over the steak. Onion may be used with small sprigs of parsley or watercress, if desired.

PORTERHOUSE STEAK

Trim off the surplus fat and place a choice porterhouse steak or sirloin steak on the preheated greased top section in the broiler pan. The meat should be cut at least 1½ inches thick for broiling. Two or 2½ inches makes a nicer steak. Put the broiler pan in the heated broiler compartment. Do not put the fork into the fiber of the meat, as the juices will escape and some of the flavor will be lost. Slip the fork into the fat at the edge and turn carefully, or turn with meat tongs. Sear this side for 5 minutes. Then lower the flame or lower the broiling pan. Broil for 15 to 20 minutes for medium well-done steak. For a steak which is desired quite rare lessen the time for broiling. Increase the length of time for a very well-done piece of meat. When the steak is removed from the broiler, season with salt and pepper. Pour off the excess fat from the broiler pan and add 2 tablespoons of hot water. Heat over a surface burner and pour over the meat on the platter just before serving. Melted butter may be used in place of the meat juice if desired.

SWEETBREADS

Wash and remove the outer skin. Parboil over a surface burner for 5 minutes in boiling water to cover. Drain and slice in halves lengthwise. Brush the top with melted butter. Place on the top section in the broiler pan and put the pan in the heated broiler compartment. Brown for 5 minutes, then turn and brown 4 minutes longer. Sweetbreads may be served on toast as an entrée or with a rich sauce.

CHICKEN

Select very young and tender chickens and have them split through the center. Clean them very thoroughly, removing the oil bag and all the hairs and pin feathers. Place each half with the skin side up on the greased top section in the broiler pan. Turn the flame low and put the pan in the heated broiler compartment. Let brown for 5 minutes, then turn every 5 minutes until the chicken is done. Tender chicken will broil in about 30 minutes.

Toast and Sandwiches

TOAST

Cut the bread ¼ inch thick. Place it on the top section in the broiler pan and place the pan in the heated broiler compartment. Brown on one side, then turn and brown on the other.

CINNAMON TOAST

2 tablespoons butter   ½ teaspoon cinnamon
2 tablespoons sugar

Brown 6 thin slices of bread on the broiler pan top section in the heated broiler compartment. Then turn and brown on the other side. Spread with butter, cinnamon and sugar which have been creamed together. Return to the broiler until the sugar is melted. This will take about half a minute.

TOASTED CRACKERS

Arrange saltines in a pan. Brush with melted butter. Sprinkle with paprika and place on the broiler pan in a previously heated compartment until the crackers have become a delicate brown. Other kinds of crackers may be substituted or the wafers may be spread with grated cheese or even thin slices of cheese and placed under the broiler flame until it melts and becomes delicately brown. These wafers may be used as an accompaniment to a salad course or with after-dinner coffee.

ENGLISH MUFFINS

Split English Muffins through the center. Place on the broiler pan top section in the heated broiler compartment and toast until a delicate brown on both sides. Butter the muffins while still hot and serve with kumquat or other tart marmalade.

SAVORY BEEF SANDWICHES

Melt the butter in a frying pan. Add thinly sliced chipped dried beef and stir over a surface burner for several minutes until the beef becomes cooked. Prepare toast in the heated broiler, allowing 2 slices of delicately toasted bread for each sandwich. Spread one side of the toast with melted butter, and between the buttered slices put the frizzled beef. Spread thinly with a mixture of horseradish and tomato catsup, using twice as much catsup as horseradish.

BAR LE DUC SANDWICHES

Spread thinly sliced pieces of bread with softened butter. Then spread with cream cheese which has been mixed with enough cream to make it spread easily. Put some bar le duc jelly on the top and cover with a second slice of buttered bread. Toast these sandwiches until they are a delicate brown by placing them on the broiler pan top section in the heated broiler compartment. Marmalade may be used instead of the bar le duc if desired.

CHEESE SANDWICHES

Cut the bread not more than ¼ inch thick. Spread with soft butter and put a thin slice of Cheddar or Swiss cheese on top. Put a second slice of thin bread, which has been buttered, on top of this and place the sandwiches on the top section in the broiler pan. Put the pan in the heated broiler compartment and toast until the outside of both pieces of bread are delicately browned. Remove from the broiler and serve while still warm.

CLUB SANDWICHES

Use 3 slices of thinly cut bread for each sandwich. Toast both sides until delicately brown in the heated broiler compartment, by placing them on the top section in the broiler pan. Butter one side of each slice while the toast is still hot. On one slice place a leaf of crisp lettuce, a slice of the white meat of chicken, and a thin slice of tomato. Spread with mayonnaise dressing. Put a slice of crisp bacon on the top. Cover with a second slice of lightly buttered toast. Add more lettuce, sliced tomato, mayonnaise and crisp bacon. Put the third slice of toast with the buttered side down over this. Garnish with slices of dill pickle or stuffed olives in a small leaf of heart lettuce. These sandwiches are served hot and are usually for the main dish at luncheon.

HAM SANDWICHES

Put the slices of ham on the top section of the broiler pan. Place this in the heated broiler compartment and broil the ham until the edges curl. Turn and broil ½ minute longer. Place a piece of the broiled ham on a buttered thin slice of bread that has been toasted on one side. Cover each sandwich with a slice of bread which has been toasted and buttered on one side.

PEANUT BUTTER SANDWICHES

Butter thin slices of bread evenly and spread peanut butter on top. Put a second slice of buttered thin bread on top and place on the top section in the broiler pan in the heated broiler compartment. Toast well on each side.

ROLLED SANDWICHES

Cut fresh bread as thin as possible. Remove crusts and lightly spread each piece with butter, then with cream or other soft cheese. Roll as for jelly roll, holding it together with skewers. Place on the broiler pan top section in the heated broiler compartment. Turn until they are entirely toasted. Remove from the pan, take out the skewers, and serve.

Dates and chopped nuts may be added to the cheese, or other soft fillings may be used. These sandwiches are especially nice for afternoon tea and can be attractively garnished with a small amount of watercress stuck in the end of each roll. They may also be used as an accompaniment for soup or salad if filled with grated Cheddar cheese.

SALAD SANDWICHES

Chop or grind left-over beef, veal or lamb. Mix with minced celery, onion and cucumber. Add enough mayonnaise dressing to moisten this mixture to a consistency which will be easy to spread. Cut 2 slices of bread about ¼ inch thick for each sandwich. Butter them lightly and spread one with the above mixture. Put a second slice of bread on the top and toast each side of the sandwiches until delicately brown by placing them on the top of the broiler pan in the heated broiler compartment.

TOMATO SANDWICHES

Butter thin slices of bread evenly and place thin slices of tomato on top. Season with salt and pepper. Put a second slice of buttered thin bread on top. Toast the sandwiches on each side on the broiler pan in the heated broiler compartment.

OPEN TOMATO AND CHEESE SANDWICHES

Cut thin slices of bread and butter them on one side. Spread with pimiento cheese and put very thin slices of tomato over the top. Season the tomatoes with salt and pepper. Dot with butter and place open sandwiches on the top section of the broiler pan. Place this in the broiler pan in the heated broiler compartment and toast until the tomato has browned and the cheese is melted.

167

Vegetables

CARROTS

Use cooked carrots. If small, leave whole. If large, cut in halves or quarters lengthwise. Place on the greased top section in the broiler pan and dot with bits of butter. Sprinkle with salt and pepper and place in the heated broiler compartment and broil for 15 minutes. They may be turned if desired, but turning is unnecessary.

MUSHROOMS

Use caps 1½ to 2 inches in diameter for broiling. Wash the fresh caps well. If necessary remove the skins. The washed skins and stems may be used for soup if desired. Place the mushroom caps on the buttered top section in the broiler pan with the tops down. Put the pan in the heated broiler compartment and broil for 5 minutes. Turn and broil the tops for another 5 minutes after sprinkling them with salt. Spread with a small piece of butter.

Broiled Mushrooms may be served as an entrée on toast with a sauce, or may be used as a garnish for meats or fish.

DUCHESS POTATOES

3 cups mashed potatoes   1 egg yolk

Add the egg yolk to the freshly mashed potatoes. Shape into round cakes or into rosettes by putting through a pastry tube. Place on the buttered top section of the broiler pan. Put the pan in the heated broiler compartment about 2 inches from the flame. Brush the top with egg white and let brown about 6 minutes. Duchess Potatoes are usually used with planked steak or fish.

HASHED BROWN POTATOES

6 cups potatoes	1 teaspoon salt
1½ teaspoons onions	⅛ teaspoon pepper
1 tablespoon parsley	3 tablespoons butter

Add the finely chopped onion, parsley, salt and pepper to the finely chopped boiled potatoes. Place in a shallow, well-buttered pan. Dot with bits of butter and place in the heated broiler compartment so that the top of the pan is about 2½ inches from the flame. Turn the flame down to half and brown for 20 minutes.

SWEET POTATOES

Remove the skins from boiled sweet potatoes and cut the potatoes into halves lengthwise. Place on the buttered top section of the broiler pan with the flat side up. Dot with bits of butter and sprinkle with salt. Place the broiler pan in the heated broiler compartment. Broil for about 15 minutes.

TOMATOES

Cut large and firm tomatoes in halves. Place them cut side up on the buttered top section in the broiler pan. Dot with bits of butter. Season with salt and pepper. Put the broiler pan in the heated broiler compartment and broil about 15 minutes.

CHAPTER XVI

LORAIN OVEN CANNING

In general, there are two types of canning, one is the open kettle method which is seldom used today. The other is the jar-cooked method which, for home canning, is most frequently employed. Jar-cooked food may be preserved by sterilizing in the Lorain Oven, a Hot Water Bath or in a Pressure Cooker.

Advantages of Canning by the Lorain Oven Method

It is an advantage to use an oven equipped with a Lorain Oven Heat Regulator for home canning. Such a piece of equipment requires no special storage space when not in use as do some other pieces of equipment which are sometimes used for canning, because it will be in daily use. Canning by the Lorain Oven Method requires no extra expenditure of time. Set the Lorain Oven Heat Regulator at the temperature desired for canning; light the gas; then with no further effort or watching, this temperature will be maintained as long as desired. It is possible to do other work while the processing is going on because it is not necessary to watch the foods.

No heavy lifting of water is necessary, and the house is not filled with steam during the time the canning is being done. It is the practical, modern, and up-to-date method of home canning.

Pressure Cooker

By the use of the Pressure Cooker it is possible to heat the food to a temperature above the boiling point of water. In a Hot Water Bath and a Lorain Controlled Oven a boiling temperature may be maintained. Complete instructions for the use of the Pressure Cooker come with the piece of equipment. Complete time tables for processing food may be secured from the pressure cooker manufacturer or from manufacturers of glass jars.

General Directions

for

Lorain Oven Canning

Before starting to can any product read these general directions for Lorain Oven Canning.

Fresh Products

The fresher the products to be canned the more nearly perfect the results will be. The flavor of fresh, firm and ripe products is superior to that of those which have been allowed to stand for some time after they have been marketed. Foods which are overripe, bruised, decayed, or blemished are more difficult to can successfully, as they contain more bacteria which must be destroyed. The fewer organisms there are present and the fewer there are to destroy the easier it is to can successfully by any method.

Bacteria and Spoilage

Foods spoil because in them or on them are tiny minute organisms called bacteria. These bacteria, when given the conditions best suited for their growth and food on which to live, will develop and grow. During the process of growth and reproduction they change our foods from substances which are useful to the body into substances which sometimes contain poisons to the body. The principle of the preservation of food is to start with foods in which there are as few of these organisms as possible so that there will be fewer to destroy, and to destroy all that are left in the food so that they will not have an opportunity to grow, spoiling the food. Then it will be possible to serve delicious canned products during seasons of the year when fresh products are not grown or in localities where they cannot be obtained.

171

Cleanliness

One of the most important factors in food preservation is the element of cleanliness. Foods should be clean to start with and then should be handled carefully in order that they will be kept clean. In this way there are fewer bacteria present. When they are present in great numbers, it is easy for them to grow and produce more bacteria or spores. Spores are highly resistant cells of bacteria which are very difficult to destroy because they can withstand higher temperatures and less favorable conditions than the other cells. Their presence makes food more difficult to can. Therefore, the cleaner it is possible to obtain foods; the cleaner it is possible to make them before canning; and the cleaner it is possible to make and keep the jars, rubbers, and all the cooking utensils with which the foods will come in contact, the more certain we are of these foods keeping an indefinite period of time after canning.

Containers

There are many types of jars which are useful for home canning. Lorain Oven Canning can be carried on successfully in any jar which you know will make a perfect seal and which will stand boiling temperatures without breaking. Any kind of jar which is to be used should be tested for perfect sealing. It sometimes happens that jars have slight imperfections either on top of the jar, or the cover may not be quite perfect. This means that even when the cover is placed on properly and with the greatest care, the imperfection may be sufficient to allow air to gain entrance into the jar. If the air gets in the jar, the bacteria which are present in it will also get in and attack the food, spoiling it for our use.

To test the jars for leaks, fill them with water and place a rubber on each jar, put the top on and tighten it. Then invert the jar and turn it around over a clean towel to see whether any of the water leaks from it. If it does not, it is likely that the jar is perfect.

All jars and tops must be clean before using. They should be scalded in boiling water for several minutes. Remove them from this boiling water just before filling. Do this by lifting them from the water with some utensil which has been scalded or something which will touch only the outside of the jar.

Some jars come with rubbers in the top. If you have used these with success for other methods of canning, you will be just as successful if the oven is used.

Fill the jars to within one inch of the top for oven canning to prevent the liquid in the jars from running over into the oven. Foods will keep just as well whether the jars are completely filled or not, and it is easier for the jar to form a perfect seal if there is a small space between the contents and the top of the jar.

Never remove the top to fill a jar if part of the liquid has evaporated. To do so will allow contaminated air to enter the jar and will doubtless cause spoilage.

Rubbers

It pays to select rubbers of good quality. If it pays to can foods for home consumption, it pays to use the best rubbers to form a perfect seal. A new rubber should be used for each jar of food which is to be canned. Just because it has been used once and seems to be good is no reason that it will stand another period of processing (subjecting to heat) or the pressure of the lid on the jar another time. Using a rubber ring a second time is a risk which is costly, for the food may spoil because of the lack of a new rubber. A good rubber will not crack when it is bent or folded or when it is stretched or pulled. It will be elastic and very firm. Rubbers, like jars, should be always cleaned in boiling water just before using.

Filling the Jars

It is unnecessary to fill jars to the very top. When they are filled too full, the liquid is apt to overflow into the oven. Starchy foods will expand during processing and if the jars have been filled too full, they may not seal properly. Some foods shrink during the period of processing due to their softening and a space may be left at the top of the jar above the surface of the food. This air space becomes sterilized by the heat of the oven and will not prevent the contents of the jar from keeping if the jar has been completely sealed.

Processing

Set the RED WHEEL at the temperature desired so that when the jars have been filled and partly sealed they may be placed at once in the heated oven. Put them far enough apart to allow for heat circulation (about 2 inches). They are then processed, or left in the heated oven at the temperature called for under the directions given for each food, for the required length of time. In this way heat is carried to the contents of the jar, cooking the food contained within and destroying the organisms which may be present. *Increase the length of the processing period 20% when canning at high altitudes.*

Sealing

Just as soon as each jar has been removed from the oven complete the seal. Different types of jars require different ways for making the seal perfect.

Perfect sealing is very important because if the jars are not entirely sealed, air will eventually gain entrance into them and this in time will cause the food to spoil.

Storing

Be sure the jars are wiped off before storing.

Label each jar with the name of its contents and the date of canning.

Store in a clean, well aired, dark, dry, and cool place (50° F.– 60° F.). Light, heat, or freezing temperatures may spoil the most carefully canned fruits and vegetables.

Look over the "preserve closet" occasionally and if any jars of food have the appearance of not keeping well remove them.

Do not use any jars of canned food which have any signs of spoilage. Discard any food which has a peculiar odor or look. Occasionally a jar of food will spoil even though it has been canned at the same time and according to the same directions as used for other jars which have kept perfectly.

BOIL ALL CANNED VEGETABLES FOR 10 MINUTES BEFORE USING.

Steps in Oven Canning

1. Select perfect, fresh foods.
2. Clean them by the best method for the particular food being canned.
3. Prepare according to specific directions given for each kind of food.
4. Test jars and rubbers.
5. Clean jars and rubbers.
6. Put clean and new rubbers on jars. Pack the food into the jars. Salt is added to vegetables. Fill to within one inch of the top with boiling water, for vegetables, or boiling syrup for fruits.
7. Place top in position and seal or partly seal. The method of sealing will depend on the kind of jar being used. It is presumed that each person will be familiar with the proper manipulation of the jars being used.
8. As soon as the jars are filled place them in the heated oven. Set the RED WHEEL at the temperature desired long enough in advance to have the oven heated when the jars are ready to go in.
9. Place the jars in the oven far enough apart to allow for circulation of heat between them (about 2 inches). The oven may be filled to capacity. If quarts are used, place them on the lower rack. If pints are used, both racks may be filled.
10. Process the length of time given in the table for each food.
11. Remove from the oven at the end of the processing period.
12. Completely seal the jars. Invert for a few minutes to be sure the seal is perfect. Do not allow them to cool in this position, as this works against the forming of the seal. Let stand until cool. If an automatic-seal jar is used, let the jar become cold and then invert it. Do not tighten screw tops after the jars have become cool. This may break the seal.
13. Cool as rapidly as possible. Rapid cooling helps to preserve color.
14. Label and date.
15. Store jars in a clean, well aired, cool, dry, and dark place.

Fruits

Canning in seasons and localities when fruits are plentiful is an advantage from the standpoint of economy. In this way it is possible to have the finest products during the time of the year when fresh fruits are not available. The delicious flavor will enhance the appeal of Lorain Oven Home Canned Fruits. They are appetizing when served just as opened from the can or when made into one of many kinds of baked desserts. Shortcakes, fruit cobblers, or fruit pies made of canned fruits add a distinction to the meal.

Hot Pack Canning

The hot pack method is advised for fruits. Simmer the fruits in syrup about 3 minutes (except berries), then pack hot into sterilized jars and add boiling syrup to within one inch of the top of the jar.

Cold Pack Canning

For cold packing the food is prepared and packed into the jars, the boiling syrup is poured over it to within one inch of the top. When this method is used the processing time should be increased 10 minutes.

SYRUP

There are three grades of syrup ordinarily used in canning fruits, namely: Thin, Medium and Thick. The thin syrups are used usually on the mild sweet fruits; the medium syrups on the tart fruits; and the heavy syrups for very acid fruits.

Syrup Table

SYRUP	SUGAR	WATER
Thin	1 measure	3 measures
Medium	1 measure	2 measures
Thick	1 measure	1 measure

This table recommended by the U. S. Dept. of Agriculture.

If desired, or for very tart fruits, an even thicker syrup than given in the above table may be made by using a larger proportion of sugar to water.

CHERRIES

Temperature, 275 degrees; Time, 35 minutes

Wash the cherries, pick them over to be sure the imperfect ones have been removed. Remove the seeds if desired. Cook them in a syrup made of 3 parts of sugar to 2 parts of water for 7 minutes. Allow the fruit to stand in this syrup over night. Pack the cherries into hot clean jars on which new clean rubbers have been adjusted. Pour boiling syrup over them to within 1 inch of the top of the jar. Partly seal, then process in a Lorain controlled oven at 275 degrees for 35 minutes. Complete the seal immediately upon removal from the oven. Canning by this method keeps the cherries distributed throughout the jars. If this is not an important factor, they can be canned by packing them immediately into jars after they have been washed and seeded. A boiling syrup can be poured over them, filling the jar to within 1 inch of the top; then process for the proper length of time and remove from the oven and complete the seal immediately. Test for leaks. Label, and store in a cool, dry place.

GOOSEBERRIES

Temperature, 275 degrees; Time, 35 minutes

Wash the berries, pick them over to be sure the imperfect ones have been removed. Remove the seeds if desired. Cook the berries in a syrup made of 3 parts of sugar to 2 parts of water for 7 minutes. Allow the gooseberries to stand in this syrup over night. Pack them into hot clean jars on which new clean rubbers have been adjusted. Pour the boiling syrup over them to within 1 inch of the top. Partly seal and process in the oven with the Lorain Regulator set at 275 degrees for 35 minutes. Complete the seal and test for leaks as soon as removed from the oven. Canning by this method keeps the gooseberries evenly distributed throughout the jars. Label, and store in a cool, dry place.

*PEACHES

Temperature, 275 degrees; Time, 35 minutes

Place the peaches in boiling water for from 1 to 3 minutes to scald. This loosens the skin and they can then be peeled much more easily. Peaches can be canned whole or cut in halves or sliced, if desired. After they have been prepared, precook in the syrup for 3 minutes and place in the jars, pour boiling syrup over them to fill the jars to within 1 inch of the top. Have clean new rubbers on the clean hot jars. Partly seal and process in the oven with the Lorain Regulator set at 275 degrees for 35 minutes. Remove from the oven; complete the seal, and test for leaks. Label, and store in a cool, dry place.

*PEARS

Temperature, 275 degrees; Time, 35 minutes

Pare the pears. They may be left whole or cut in halves and the seeds and cores removed. Pack them quickly in the clean hot jars on which clean new rubbers have been adjusted. Pour a boiling syrup over the pears to fill the jars to within 1 inch of the top. If the pears are of a very hard variety, put them in the boiling syrup on the surface burner, letting them boil for 5 minutes in this syrup. Then pack them in the jars and pour the hot syrup over them. Partly seal and process in the oven at 275 degrees for 35 minutes. Remove from the oven; complete the seal, and test for leaks. Label, and store in a cool, dry place.

---

*NOTE: As these fruits discolor very easily when they come in contact with the air, they should be packed into the jars very quickly after they are pared and the boiling syrup poured over them to exclude the air. If it is not practical to do this put the fruits into water to cover, in which 1 tablespoon of salt has been added for each quart of water.

PINEAPPLE

Temperature, 275 degrees; Time, 45 minutes

Peel the pineapple. Cut it in pieces or cut in rounds and remove the core afterward. Precook in the syrup for 3 minutes, then pack into clean hot jars on which clean new rubbers have been adjusted. Add 1 tablespoon of lemon juice to each quart. Cover with a boiling syrup made of equal parts of sugar and water. If fruit is desired less sweet, make a medium or thin syrup to suit the taste (see p. 176 for proportions). Partly seal and process in the oven with the Lorain Regulator set at 275 degrees for 45 minutes. Remove from the oven; complete the seal immediately, and test for leaks. Label, and store in a cool, dry place.

PLUMS

Temperature, 275 degrees; Time, 45 minutes

Wash fresh firm fruit. Prick the skin of each plum in several places. This sometimes prevents the skins from bursting. It is not necessary to remove the skins. If plums are very tart use a thick syrup (see p. 176 for proportions). Precook in the syrup for 3 minutes, then pack in hot, scalded jars which have had clean new rubbers adjusted on them. Fill to within 1 inch of the top with boiling hot syrup. Adjust the lid loosely. Place in the Lorain controlled oven with the regulator set at 275 degrees for 45 minutes. At the end of this period remove from the oven; complete the seal, and test for leaks. Label, and store in a cool, dry place.

RASPBERRIES

Temperature, 275 degrees; Time, 35 minutes

Wash the berries and select only the perfect ones. Pack into jars and pour boiling syrup over them or cook them in a syrup made of 3 parts of sugar to 2 parts of water for 7 minutes. Allow the berries to stand in this syrup over night. The berries will absorb the syrup. This makes them heavier and they are less likely to float to the top of the jar. Pack them into clean hot jars on which clean new rubbers have been adjusted. Cover with boiling syrup to within 1 inch of the top. Partly seal and process in the oven with the Lorain Regulator set at 275 degrees for 35 minutes. Complete the seal, and test for leaks. Label, and store in a cool, dry place.

STRAWBERRIES

Temperature, 275 degrees; Time, 35 minutes

Wash the berries, stem them and select only the firm perfect berries. Pack into the jars and pour boiling syrup over them or cook them in a syrup made of 3 parts of sugar to 2 parts of water for 7 minutes. Allow the berries to stand in this syrup over night. The berries will absorb the syrup. This makes them heavier and they are less likely to float to the top of the jar. Pack them loosely into clean hot jars on which clean new rubbers have been adjusted. Reheat the syrup and pour over the berries to within 1 inch of the top of the jar. Partly seal; and process in the oven with the Lorain Regulator set at 275 degrees for 35 minutes. Remove from the oven; complete the seal, and test for leaks. Label, and store in a cool, dry place.

Pickles, Relishes and Fruit Butters

Preserving by the Lorain Oven Method is an advantage especially if the product being preserved would otherwise require long cooking on the top of the stove and, therefore, would necessitate constant watching and stirring to prevent it from sticking and burning. Pickles, relishes, and fruit butters can be placed in the Lorain controlled oven and boiled slowly without watching or stirring and with no danger of the products burning. This is a relief from the drudgery of preserving and pickling by the ordinary method and makes the work easier.

APPLE BUTTER

Temperature, 350 degrees; Time, 4½ hours

1 peck apples	1½ pounds sugar
2 quarts boiled cider	1 teaspoon salt
1 ounce stick cinnamon	

Core, pare and quarter the apples. Add the cider and cinnamon and bring to the boiling point on the surface burner. The cinnamon can be tied in a small piece of clean cheese cloth and removed just before the apple butter is placed in the jars. Place in a Lorain controlled oven at 350 degrees and process for 4 hours in an open pan. At the end of this time add the sugar and salt and stir until they are thoroughly dissolved. Put into clean hot jars on which new and clean rubbers have been adjusted. Partly seal and return to the oven for 30 minutes. Remove and complete the seal. Label, and store in a cool, dry place.

CHILI SAUCE

Temperature, 350 degrees; Time, 5 hours
then
Temperature, 275 degrees; Time, 20 minutes

1 peck ripe tomatoes	1 tablespoon whole allspice
10 medium onions	1 tablespoon cloves
4 red peppers	1 tablespoon whole cinnamon
3 bunches celery	3 cups sugar
1 quart vinegar	2 tablespoons salt

Scald, peel, and chop tomatoes and put in colander to drain. Chop all the vegetables. Mix all ingredients together and heat to the boiling point on the surface burner in an open kettle. Place in the oven with the Lorain Regulator set at 350 degrees for 5 hours. Remove from the oven at the end of this period and pack into clean hot jars on which new clean rubbers have been adjusted. Partly seal and return to the oven at 275 degrees for 20 minutes. Remove from the oven and complete the seal. If bottles have been used instead of jars press corks firmly into bottle and dip the mouth of the bottle into melted paraffin several times. Label, and store in a cool, dry place.

ORANGE MARMALADE

Temperature, 350 degrees; Time, 3 hours

8 oranges (Floridas) 4 pounds

4 lemons, 1 pound

1 grapefruit, 1¼ pounds

½ as much water by measure as fruit

Equal parts sugar and cooked fruit

Wash the fruit and slice very thin. Measure and add half as much water as fruit and let stand overnight. In the morning heat it on the surface burner until it reaches the boiling point, then put it in the oven at 350 degrees for 2 hours. Measure and add an equal amount of sugar and heat again. Return to the oven at 350 degrees for 1 hour. Remove from the oven and pour into clean glasses. When cold seal with a thin layer of melted paraffin. As the paraffin hardens it shrinks away from the edge so add a little more to seal the edge.

Yield: Fourteen 8-ounce glasses.

PEACHES (Spiced)

Temperature, 275 degrees; Time, 35 minutes

4 quarts peaches
1 pint vinegar
2 pounds sugar

¼ ounce whole cloves
½ ounce stick cinnamon,
   if desired

Pour a syrup made of the vinegar, sugar, and cinnamon over the peaches which have been peeled, stuck with cloves, and packed into clean hot jars on which new clean rubbers have been adjusted. Partly seal and place in a Lorain controlled oven with the RED WHEEL set at 275 degrees for 35 minutes. Remove from the oven and complete the seal. Label, and store in a cool, dry place.

Other fruits may be spiced in the same way.

PEPPER RELISH

Temperature, 275 degrees; Time, 1½ hours

1 dozen green peppers
1 dozen red peppers
2 quarts vinegar
1 dozen medium onions, chopped

1 bunch celery,
   chopped
3 tablespoons salt
3 pounds sugar

Chop or grind the peppers. Pour boiling water over them and drain. Make a syrup of the vinegar and sugar. Add the vegetables and the salt to the syrup and bring to the boiling point over a surface burner. Place at once in the Lorain controlled oven for 1 hour at 275 degrees. Then pour into hot clean jars on which new and clean rubbers have been adjusted. Partly seal and return to the oven for 30 minutes. Remove from the oven and complete the seal. Label, and store in a cool, dry place.

WATERMELON PICKLES

Temperature, 350 degrees; Time, 1 hour
then
Temperature, 275 degrees; Time, 1 hour

For each quart use:

3 pounds watermelon rind	**1 quart water**
3 tablespoons salt	

Thoroughly wash the watermelon rind and cut it into small pieces. Soak over night in a solution made by adding 3 tablespoons of salt to 1 quart of water. In the morning remove from the brine, drain, and cook until tender in clean water. Add the rind to the hot syrup and bring to the boiling point.

Syrup

4 cups sugar	2 tablespoons stick cinnamon,
2 cups water	broken
2 cups vinegar	2 tablespoons whole cloves
1 lemon, sliced thin	2 tablespoons allspice berries

Make a syrup by cooking the sugar, water and vinegar together.

Tie the lemon and spices in a cheese cloth. Let the spice bag stay in the syrup while the pickles are boiling both on the top burner and in the oven. The spices can then be easily removed when the pickles are packed into the jars. Process in the open kettle in the oven at 350 degrees for 1 hour and pack into clean hot jars on which new and clean rubbers have been adjusted. Pour the syrup over the rind to within 1 inch of the top of the jars. Partly seal and process in the oven at 275 degrees for 1 hour. Remove from the oven and complete the seal. Label, and store in a cool, dry place.

Soups

Every well stocked emergency shelf should contain some cans of soup. They may be canned by the Lorain Oven Method with little trouble or expense.

VEGETABLE SOUP

(Without Meat Stock)

Temperature, 275 degrees; Time, 3 hours

2 cups celery	1 onion
3 cups beans	1 tablespoon salt
2 cups corn	½ teaspoon pepper
2 cups carrots	4 cups boiling water
3 cups tomatoes	

Prepare the vegetables by washing and cutting them into small pieces. Add the seasonings and water. Heat over a surface burner to the boiling point. Pack into clean hot jars with new and clean rubbers adjusted on them. Partly seal and place in a Lorain controlled oven at 275 degrees. At the end of 3 hours remove and complete the seal. Test for leaks. Label, and store in a cool, dry place.

Yield: About 5 pints.

VEGETABLE SOUP

(With Meat Stock)

Temperature, 275 degrees; Time, 3½ hours

1 pound beef round	1 onion
1 cup celery	1 pint boiling water
¾ cup carrots	1 tablespoon salt
1 cup tomato purée	½ teaspoon pepper
½ cup tomato pulp	

Sear the meat on the surface burner. Add clean vegetables cut fine, boiling water, and seasonings. Bring to the boiling point on a surface burner. Pack into clean hot jars on which clean new rubbers have been adjusted. Partly seal and place in a Lorain controlled oven at 275 degrees. At the end of 3½ hours remove and complete the seal. Test for leaks. Label, and store in a cool, dry place.

Yield: About 3 pints.

Vegetables

Only people who have used home canned vegetables canned fresh from the gardens can appreciate the fine flavor of these products. A well-stocked cupboard of canned goods provides every family with an emergency shelf for winter use. The Lorain Oven Method of canning vegetables is so practical and easy, so modern and up-to-date, that wherever it is possible to obtain very fresh vegetables there should be an adequate supply of them, Lorain Oven Canned.

Success in canning is more certain if two teaspoons of lemon juice or vinegar are added to each pint of asparagus, corn and spinach, or other greens.

ASPARAGUS

Temperature, 275 degrees; Time, 2½ hours

For each quart use:

1¼ pounds asparagus   4 teaspoons lemon juice
1 teaspoon salt   1¾ cups boiling water

Wash the asparagus well and scrape the stalks. Remove scales. Cut off tough ends. Tie same lengths together or cut into pieces of an inch in length. Put in boiling water. Boil (precook) for 5 minutes. Remove from the water and pack into clean hot jars on which new clean rubbers have been adjusted. Add the 1 teaspoon of salt and the lemon juice and cover with boiling water to within 1 inch of the top. Place the jars in the oven with the regulator set at 275 degrees and allow them to remain there for 2½ hours. Remove from the oven at the end of this period and complete the seal. Test for leaks and place where they will cool as rapidly as possible. Label, and store in a cool, dry place.

BEANS (Green)

Temperature, 275 degrees; Time, 2½ hours

For each quart use:

1 pound green beans   1¾ cups boiling water
1 teaspoon salt

Wash the beans and remove the ends and strings. Cut into inch pieces, or leave whole, and put into a pan of boiling water. Boil on the surface burner for 5 minutes. Pack loosely into clean hot jars on which new clean rubbers have been adjusted. Add the salt and fill to within 1 inch of the tops with boiling water. Partly seal. Place in a Lorain Controlled Oven at 275 degrees. At the end of 2½ hours remove from the oven and complete the seal. Test for leaks. Cool as rapidly as possible. Label, and store in a cool, dry place.

BEANS (Lima)

Temperature, 275 degrees; Time, 3 hours

For each quart use:

1¼ pounds lima beans   1½ cups boiling water
1 teaspoon salt

Wash the beans after they have been shelled. Use young and tender and very fresh beans if possible. Put them in boiling water and boil (precook) for 5 minutes. Drain off the water and pack into clean hot jars on which new and clean rubbers have been adjusted. Pack them loosely into the jar; add the salt and fill with boiling water to within 1 inch of the tops. The water should come up to the top of the beans. Partly seal, place in the Lorain Controlled Oven at 275 degrees and at the end of 3 hours remove from the oven. Complete the seal; test for leaks, and place where they will cool as rapidly as possible. Label, and store in a cool, dry place.

BEANS (Yellow)

Temperature, 275 degrees; Time, 2½ hours

For each quart use:

1 pound yellow beans   1¾ cups boiling water
1 teaspoon salt

Wash the beans, remove the ends and strings. Cut into 1 inch pieces or leave whole. Place in a pan of boiling water and boil for 5 minutes. Put new and clean rubbers on the jars which are clean and scalding hot. Add the salt and fill to within 1 inch of the tops with boiling water. Partly seal. Place in a Lorain Controlled Oven at 275 degrees and at the end of 2½ hours remove from the oven, complete the seal, and test for leaks. Cool as rapidly as possible. Label, and store in a cool, dry place.

BEETS

Temperature, 275 degrees; Time, 2½ hours

For each quart use:

10 or 12 whole small beets   1 teaspoon salt
(1 pound, if sliced)   Boiling water

Wash the beets well, brushing with a vegetable brush. Put in a pan of boiling water and boil for 15 minutes. Dip in cold water to make the beets easier to handle. Remove the skins. Leave whole or slice and pack into clean hot jars on which clean new rubbers have been adjusted. Add the salt and boiling water to fill the jars to within 1 inch of the tops. Partly seal. Place in an oven the temperature of which is 275 degrees and process for 2½ hours. At the end of this period remove them from the oven and complete the seal. Test for leaks and cool as rapidly as possible to preserve the color. Label, and store in a cool, dry place.

CARROTS

Temperature, 275 degrees; Time, 2½ hours

For each quart use:

1 pound carrots
1 teaspoon salt

1½ cups boiling water

Wash young and tender carrots. Scrape if desired. It is not necessary to scrape the very young carrots although some people prefer to have the outside skin removed before canning. The carrots may be cut lengthwise into quarters, sliced or packed whole. Boil for 5 minutes. If desired cut they should be cut before they are put in the pan of water on the top of the stove to boil. Pack the carrots loosely in the hot clean jars on which new clean rubbers have been adjusted. Add the salt and boiling water to within 1 inch of the tops. Partly seal and place in a Lorain Controlled Oven at 275 degrees for 2½ hours. At the end of this period remove from the oven, complete the seal, and test the jars for leaks. Cool as rapidly as possible. Label, and store in a cool, dry place.

CORN

Temperature, 275 degrees; Time, 3 hours

For each quart use:

3 cups corn
1 teaspoon salt

4 teaspoons lemon juice
¾ cup boiling water

Place husked ears of young and tender corn in boiling water to cover. Let boil for 5 minutes. Remove from boiling water and cut from the cob. Pack loosely into hot clean jars on which new clean rubbers have been adjusted. Add the salt and lemon juice and fill the jars to within 1 inch of the tops with boiling water. Partly seal and place in a Lorain Controlled Oven at 275 degrees and at the end of 3 hours remove from the oven, complete the seal and test for leaks. Cool as rapidly as possible. Label, and store in a cool, dry place.

PEAS

Temperature, 275 degrees; Time, 3 hours

For each quart use:

1¼ pounds peas   1½ cups boiling water
1 teaspoon salt

Shell tender and young green peas. Wash and boil on the surface burner for 5 minutes in enough boiling water to cover. Remove from the water and pack loosely into clean hot jars. Have new and clean rubbers adjusted on the jars. Add the salt and fill the jars to within 1 inch of the tops with boiling water, and partly seal. Place in a Lorain Controlled Oven at 275 degrees and at the end of 3 hours remove from the oven, complete the seal, and test for leaks. Cool as rapidly as possible. Label, and store in a cool, dry place.

SPINACH

Temperature, 275 degrees; Time, 3 hours

For each quart use:

1½ pounds spinach   4 teaspoons lemon juice
1 teaspoon salt   1 cup boiling water

Spinach requires especially thorough washing since the little veins of the leaves are apt to hold dirt. The stem ends and all discoloration from the edges of the leaves must be removed. When this has been done cook the spinach for 5 minutes in a covered pan on the surface burner using just enough boiling water to prevent burning. Remove from this water. Pack loosely into hot scalded jars on which the clean new rubbers have been adjusted. Add the salt, lemon juice and the boiling water to within 1 inch of the tops. Partly seal. Place in a Lorain Controlled Oven at 275 degrees and at the end of 3 hours remove from the oven, complete the seal, and test for leaks. Cool as rapidly as possible. Label, and store in a cool, dry place.

Prepare other greens the same way.

190

SQUASH

Temperature, 275 degrees; Time, 3 hours

For each quart use:

Squash   1 teaspoon salt

Use young and tender squash which has been thoroughly washed and cut it in pieces. Bake at 400 degrees until soft. This will take from 1 hour to 1 hour and 20 minutes, depending on the hardness of the squash. Remove from the shell and pack loosely into clean hot jars on which new clean rubbers have been adjusted. Add the salt and partly seal. Do not cover with boiling water. Put in the Lorain Controlled Oven at 275 degrees for 3 hours. At the end of this time remove from the oven and complete the seal. Cool as rapidly as possible. Label, and store in a cool, dry place.

TOMATOES

Temperature, 275 degrees; Time, 45 minutes

For each quart use:

Tomatoes   Boiling water
1 teaspoon salt

Scald perfect tomatoes by dipping them in boiling water for several minutes. Do not boil the water after the tomatoes have been placed in it. Let them stay in 3 minutes. Remove from water and peel. They can be handled easier if they are dipped in cold water first. Pack them into clean jars on which new clean rubbers have been adjusted, using enough tomatoes to fill each jar. No amount can be given as it depends on whether the tomatoes are desired whole or quartered or whether just the pulp is wanted.

If tomatoes are canned whole, skin them and pack into clean jars on which new clean rubbers have been adjusted. Add the salt and fill with boiling water to within one inch of the tops.

If it does not matter whether they remain whole or are broken fill the spaces between the tomatoes with tomato pulp. This is done by pressing the softer tomatoes into the jar. Do not fill the jar too full. Partly seal. Place in a Lorain Controlled Oven at 275 degrees for 45 minutes. At the end of this time remove and complete the seal. Test for leaks and cool as rapidly as possible. Label, and store in a cool, dry place.

TIME TABLE FOR
LORAIN OVEN CANNING

Product	Temperature	Time
Fruits (Hot Pack)		
Cherries	275°	35 min.
Gooseberries	275°	35 min.
Peaches	275°	35 min.
Pears	275°	35 min.
Pineapple	275°	45 min.
Plums	275°	45 min.
Raspberries	275°	35 min.
Strawberries	275°	35 min.

Pickles, Relishes and Fruit Butters

Apple Butter	350°	4½ hrs.
Chili Sauce	350°	5 hrs.
	then	
	275°	20 min.
Orange Marmalade	350°	3 hrs.
Peaches, Spiced	275°	35 min.
Pepper Relish	275°	1½ hrs.
Watermelon Pickles	350°	1 hr.
	then	
	275°	1 hr.

Soups

Vegetable Soup (Without meat stock)	275°	3 hrs.
Vegetable Soup (With meat stock)	275°	3½ hrs.

Vegetables

Asparagus	275°	2½ hrs.
Beans, Green	275°	2½ hrs.
Beans, Lima	275°	3 hrs.
Beans, Yellow	275°	2½ hrs.
Beets	275°	2½ hrs.
Carrots	275°	2½ hrs.
Corn	275°	3 hrs.
Peas	275°	3 hrs.
Spinach	275°	3 hrs.
Squash	275°	3 hrs.
Tomatoes	275°	45 min.

TIME AND TEMPERATURE CHART

FOR

LORAIN OVEN COOKING

Product	Temperature	Time
Apples, Baked or Scalloped.............	400°	30–40 min.
Beans, Boston Baked..................	300°	6 hrs.
Beef, Roast, Tender Cuts (uncovered pan) Tough Cuts (covered pan, valve open in cover, boiling water in bottom of pan)—SEAR at....................	500°	20–30 min., then
BAKE at..................	275°	3 hrs.
Biscuits, Baking Powder...............	450°	14–16 min.
Bread, Boston Brown (hot water surrounding)..................................	275°	3 hrs.
Bread, Nut, and other Baking Powder Loaf	350°	45–60 min.
Bread, Yeast...........................	450°	15 min., then
	375°	45 min., or
	375°	1 hr.
Cake, Coffee, or Coffee Bread............	400°	20 min.
Cake, Angel Food or Sponge	325°	1 hr.
Cake, Chocolate Layer.................	350°	35–40 min.
Cake, Chocolate Cup..................	375°	15–18 min.
Cake, Butter Sponge...................	350°	35–40 min.
Cake, containing butter, Loaf...........	350°	55–60 min.
Cake, containing butter, Layer..........	375°	30–35 min.
Cake, containing butter, Cup...........	375°	18–20 min.
Cake, Fruit...........................	275°	3 hrs.
Cake, Gold, Loaf......................	325°	60–65 min.
Cake, Pound, Loaf....................	325°	2 hrs.
Chicken, Roast—SEAR at..............	500°	20 min., then
BAKE at..............	275°	28–30 min. per lb.
Chicken, Stewed......................	275°	3 hrs.

194

Product	Temperature	Time
Chili con Carne	300°	3½ hrs.
Chops, Baked	400°	50 min.
Cookies, Plain	375°	10–15 min.
Baked Fudge	350°	40–45 min.
Chocolate Cocoanut Cakes	350°	15 min.
Cocoanut Dainties	375°	10–12 min.
Date Bars	350°	30 min.
Drop Cakes	375°	12–15 min.
Ginger Wafers	375°	6– 8 min.
Lady Fingers	350°	10 min.
Macaroons	325°	20 min.
Nut Meringues	275°	35–40 min.
Pecan Squares	350°	25 min.
Rocks	350°	18 min.
Corn Pudding, Baked (hot water surrounding)	400°	40 min.
Cream Puff Shells, large	450°	20 min., then
	325°	20 min.
Custard (hot water surrounding)	350°	40 min.
Custard, Cup (hot water surrounding)	350°	30–35 min.
Fish, Baked, Stuffed	400°	1 hr.
Fish, Fillet	450°	25 min.
Fruit, Stewed	400°	1 hr.
Gingerbread	350°	40–45 min.
Ham, Baked without water—SEAR at	500°	20–30 min., then
BAKE at	275°	4 hrs.
Lamb, Roast (uncovered pan, no water added)—SEAR at	500°	20–30 min., then
BAKE at	275°	3 hrs., or
	350°	30 min., per lb.
Meringue, on Pies	300°	15–20 min.
Muffins	400°	25–30 min.
Muffins, Potato Flour	375°	20 min.
Pie Shells (without filling)	450°	12–15 min.
Pie (with one crust and with uncooked filling, such as custard)	450°	10 min., then
	325°	30 min.

Product	Temperature	Time
Pie, Two Crusts	425°	35–40 min.
Popovers	450°	25 min., then
	350°	15 min.
Pork, Roast (uncovered pan)—SEAR at	500°	20–30 min., then
BAKE at	275°	3 hrs.
Potatoes, Baked	450°	50–60 min.
Potatoes, Scalloped	400°	50–60 min.
Pudding, Indian	400°	30 min.
Puddings, Steamed	400°	1 hr., or
	275°	3 hrs.
Rolls, Parker House	400°	15–20 min.
Soufflés	325°	1 hr.
Soups	275°	3 hrs.
Steak, Baked—SEAR at	500°	20 min., then
BAKE at	275°	30–35 min.
Stews, Meat—SEAR at	500°	20–30 min., then
BAKE at	275°	3 hrs.
Toast, Melba	325°	15–18 min.
Turkey, or Goose, Roast (covered pan, valve open in cover, boiling water in bottom of pan)—SEAR at	500°	20–30 min., then
BAKE at	275°	15–20 min. per lb.
Veal, Roast (covered pan, valve open in cover, boiling water in bottom of pan)—SEAR at	500°	20–30 min., then
BAKE at	275°	3 hrs.
Vegetables	400°	dependent on kind
Whole Meals	275°	3 hrs.

INDEX

INDEX